A Glance of **Tawau** in the **Sixties**

A Glance of **Tawau** in the **Sixties**

Land Below the Wind

BRYAN PAUL LAI

PARTRIDGE
A Penguin Random House Company

To order additional copies of this book, contact
Toll Free 800 101 2657 (Singapore)
Toll Free 1 800 81 7340 (Malaysia)
orders.singapore@partridgepublishing.com

www.partridgepublishing.com/singapore

Contents

Contents

Acknowledgement

I wrote this book as a follow up of my previous book "the joy of life", a gesture of goodwill to preserve some of the facts happening in Tawau as seen personally by me since 1963 to 1998. It was an external observation as I saw it with my own eyes of past events in Tawau, from a small village to a metropolitan town. I would like to express my appreciation to Marguerite my daughter for her comments and proof reading of the articles. My very sincere thanks to all those that allowed me to use some pictures that portrayed in this book, particularly to Mary Domingo, Mr Francis Anthony, Mary Lu, Annie Hee, George Chang, Mr Colin Rose previously attached to the British air defence squadron in Tawau in 1965, Rev Fr Parson of Holy Trinity Church and all those that in one way provided me all the information as stated in the record. In case of certain discrepancy or in one way or another hurt anyone's feeling due to misspelt in names, please accept my apology.

Hopefully this simple book will rekindle all the past memories that Tawau offered as the town grew into a beautiful future city.

Episode 1

(1963)

The shadows of destiny

$\mathcal{I}$ stirred, and just for a split second, managed to gain consciousness for a while, only to be lost to the world again. The next time I woke up, I felt the chill in the room. I opened my eyes, only to find myself in a weird place. I looked up and managed to make out the many ominous and strange faces looking at me. I saw my father standing beside my mother, both looking at me with concerned faces.

My thoughts began to wander around, seeking answers and desperately trying to figure out what was happening, and why was I in this room with people who looked like doctors and nurses around. Questions began to dance in my head, part of me earnestly pacifying myself that this has been just a terrible dream. When I failed to find the answers, I gave up and decided to wait for the moment to wake up quickly from this frightening affair. Unfortunately, it was all in vain and I had to admit to myself that I was not merely having a nightmare.

I tried to move, only to realize that my limbs were under siege. I tried once again to open one of my eyes slowly as it hurts to do so. I recalled seeing the ceiling fan above me, turning at a dawdling pace, squeaking at every turn as though each of its movements hurt too. My eyes finally rested on my mother's face, a blurry image at first, and seconds later, her tired and troubled face emerged distinctly looking at me with a distressed expression.

As she gazed at me, I could clearly see the worried lines etched on her forehead, but with a calm appearance, an expression that I had never seen since I was a child. As a woman of strong faith, she bowed her head in prayer, beseeching God to intervene in this moment of tragedy. I felt the touch of her tender hand on my brow. Then I was again lost in the world of oblivion.

The next morning, I woke very early in the morning. I realized that I felt a little better. Then I saw my brother Daniel for the first time, sleeping in the hospital bed next to my bed with his head bandaged. I tried to recollect the events that led us to this predicament. It was quite traumatic, and automatically, my mind blanked out again, refusing to let me recall the incident. However, I was feeling more upbeat and knew that whatever it was, my brother and I would be in good hands at this hospital.

The flower garden and the clouds above could easily be seen through the French collapsing door next to my bed. The gentle cool breeze caressed my face tenderly, comforting me, as I gaze at the sparrows flying amongst the morning glory, chirping away cheerfully as they went about their morning ritual. This blissful moment was interrupted by a nurse that came in to give me a routine checkup.

I tried to move again, struggling desperately, using my hands to pull myself up, but in vain. My mother and the nurse came to my rescue, and with their firm but tender hands, propped me up, releasing the pressure that had been building in my back. As soon as I managed to sit up, images of the tragic event that had led us to be in this place began to surface. I quickly glanced at my left, where my brother Daniel was still motionless, and on my right, I saw another guy sleeping on the bed. Later, I learnt that it was the guy who had hit us with his big bike. He was also warded, but his injuries were not as serious as ours.

Although my mind was still in a state of fuzziness, I managed to recall the events that led to our disaster. My brother Daniel and I were returning home, riding on a Vespa scooter that belonged to my dad. We were not wearing our safety helmets. We were just about to reach home, crossing the crossroads between Kuhara and Apas Road. Out of the blue, a big bike suddenly crossed our path. In that instant, the impact threw us off our bikes and we landed yards away, inside a shallow muddy drain. The grass and mud in the trench saved us from severe injuries to our fragile bodies or even from probable instant death.

A woman by the name of Mrs. Lucy Kau, was resting at her house balcony waiting her husband to return from work in town. Mr. Andrew Kau, Lucy's husband was the first non European to hold the post of manager of NBT Tawau. She witnessed the whole incident that had transpired. Within seconds, the crowd from the nearby houses began to assemble at the scene of the accident, looking at us in disbelief and presumed that we were both gone as there were no signs of any body movements.

The Vespa before the accident

At that time, our new house was just a hundred yards away, next to John Chin's family and the Kau family (Site of the present Promenade Hotel). Mum was in the kitchen preparing lunch. She heard the commotion and immediately went to the window to see what had transpired. The crowd was getting bigger and to satisfy her curiosity, she went out to join the crowd. In an instant, she recognized the scooter which laid mangled at the roadside and saw her two sons motionless in the drain.

Mom was horrified. With the help of some bystanders, she lifted us out of the drain. She did not burst into tears, but calmly addressed the situation well. We were immediately rushed to the civil hospital in town just in the nick of time before trauma sets in. The local civil ambulance service was far from perfect. It took the ambulance some time before reaching at the Apas junction, which was just around two kilometres away. Communication during those days was very primitive.

I was in and out of coma for two days. It was only on the third day that I came out of my unconsciousness and came to terms with my plight.

My brother Daniel had a slight head injury and was operated on the same day to release a blood clot. I nearly lost my left eye, but was fortunate that only a portion of my upper eyebrow was ripped off.

The Tawau civil hospital was equipped for minor operations and at that time, a surgeon from the United Kingdom was available at the civil hospital to cater for the populace of Tawau. He was a skilful surgeon who had years of experience before being sent to North Borneo. His presence gave us the assertion of proper health care.

He did a simple graft on my upper eye by slicing off a bit of my flesh from the thigh. It was not cosmetically perfect, but moderately acceptable.

Both of us were interned for five long weeks. The first week had been the most horrendous time for our parents, having to care for us and also those at home. Beside the two of us, there were four more of my brothers and sisters to care for, particularly for their schooling and daily needs. The last four weeks of our stay at the hospital had been reasonably good, as we were recovering well.

Our parents were comforted and felt calmed after the period of uncertainty. The local hospital, in spite of its modest and frugal medical supplies, provided reasonable care to us and gave us appropriate attention. Visitors came at odd hours as there was no restriction and Peter, a Timorese by birth, was the hospital attendant entrusted to clean the area every day. He became our good companion and gave us all the help that we needed.

Peter was reasonably stout and he had curly hair and a protruding eye. Due to his unusual look, children were not too comfortable to be around with him. He could only see with his right eye. He lost the other eye during a tribal conflict in his former country in Timor before migrating to North Borneo to seek for greener pasture. He had been working in the hospital for many years as an attendant. It was his duty to ensure the cleanliness of the second class ward. He arrived promptly every morning to clean the ward and to mop the floor. As he performed his duties, he took some time to chat with us and always inquired whether we needed any coffee or meat buns for breakfast. A 'tausa pau' cost fifteen cents and a 'chu yuk pau' cost only twenty five cents at that time. Now it cost RM 1.70 and RM 3.50 what a big hike!

Our ward was strategically located with a full view of the garden, an open ground with flowers and shrubs planted in neat rows. The Girl Guides, the St John and Red Cross of Holy Trinity had their weekly meeting on Saturday afternoon at a small hut just beside the government administrative office, near the hospital. The hut was normally utilized by all the association for their daily activities and meetings. When I was a scout in the year 1957 attached to the first Scout troop of SK Bandar under Cikgu Piut, Cikgu Abidin Kreah and Cikgu Ahmad Awang, the hut was our meeting area. In my patrol leader was Ishak Awadan. Normally, the guides would drop by to visit us after their training session.

Their weekly visit brought us some comfort which helped to cheer us up and expedite our healing process. The St Clare convent girls came on Sunday to console us in our solitude and prayers for our speedy recovery. As a result of the many guests, our table was always full of cookies and fruits. Mum commented that we could start a small grocery store. I gave most of them to Peter, the hospital attendance. He was so grateful that any help we required were always promptly dealt with.

At long last, after the five weeks of our stay we were given the clean bill of health and were allowed to return home.

After expressing our gratitude and thanks to the staff around, we headed for home. During the journey, dad was silent and not uttered a word till we reached home.

The moment we arrived home, dad went back to the office. At that moment, my first impulse was to locate and to see the extent of damage the accident had incurred to the scooter.

In spite of searching the whole house compound, I could not locate it. I was then told by mom that dad had given it to Ah Sung (Mr. Lee), the taxi driver who was staying just opposite the road further down. Dad had decided that he would never allow us to use a bike or scooter anymore.

For the last one week, we had some difficulty trying to bring us back to our normal routine. However, with the love and understanding from our parents, brothers and sisters, we finally managed to gain our health back and our self-confidence and tried not to recall the misfortune that had happened several weeks ago.

Daniel, my brother, who was in the lower class continued with his studies at Holy Trinity Secondary School Tawau Sabah.

I was somewhat reluctant to continue with my studies and was prepared to find a suitable job. Most of my classmates after their junior Cambridge were now all working and after missing months of study, I was prepared to leave school and seek for a job.

Dad made a courtesy call to meet Rev. Father Hurly, the school principal of Holy Trinity Secondary School. After a cordial discussion, Father Hurly expressed his opinion and told dad that it was an arduous task for me to keep up with my lessons. He advised dad that I should get a job instead. The outcome brought some relief to me as this was what I was longing for. With that conclusion, the reality of life had now begun for the next stage of my life. With no regret, I had to embark on self-improvement and face the challenging world ahead. I sat for my Cambridge several years later.

The town Wallace Bay that Peter worked for ten years
for Bombey Burma Trading Co. before retiring in 1961

My father, Peter retired from the Bombay Burma Trading Corporation in the year 1961. Immediately after that, he was engaged by Doctor Wolfe to work for him temporary at his clinic. Doctor J. Wolfe, a prominent physician came from Europe and had been in Sabah for many years with a permanent resident status.

Our new house which was close to the Holy Trinity Catholic Church was not ready and we had to rent a house a few kilometers away along Jalan Kuhara. The house belonged to the Lim family. Next to us, a European family rented a house that belonged to Mr. Lo.

One day, I was just about to finish my food when a strong, loud bang suddenly interrupted my lunch. I looked out of the window and saw that the neighbour's stilt wooden house had collapsed. The English woman living there was shaken and traumatized as she slowly emerged from the fallen building. Mom and I quickly went over to her and brought her to our house and treated her for shock and comforted her till her husband arrived...

During the course of my dad's work, he met a planter by the name of Mr. John Anselmi... He was a director and in charge of the management of the Bergosong Estate on Sebatik Island and had been in Sabah for many years. His wife was called Jacky and they had two beautiful children.

Their friendly encounter and casual talk led to some amiable interest. In a span of several weeks, they met several times to discuss in details the planned business enterprise proposed by John Anselmi. I had no idea of what transpired between the two, until John came to the house and thrash out in details the formation of a company.

My dad Peter listened with great interest, but with caution. After several meetings, they agreed to form a company called 'Service and Trading'. I was looking for a job, but had not started my quest yet..

During their final discussion, John turned to me and asked whether I was interested to work for the new company. I looked at dad for his reaction, but his body language was enough to convince me of his acceptance. The company was finally formed and license and other relevant documents were obtained from the local authorities.

Service and Trading in Tawau Town

The proposed shop which had been earmarked belonged to Mr. Teo. It was situated close to the Charted Bank at Jalan Chester. With some additional shelves and slight renovation, the shop was ready for occupation. Mr. John Anselmi, Peter's partner, took a trip to Singapore. Without consulting Peter, he ordered from a company called C. K. Tang, an assortment of goods, such as household and kitchen wares, bottles of perfume and various other items without ensuring that those items were suitable for the Tawau market.

It kept us busy for several weeks to keep track of all the goods. Finally, it was laid on display on the shelf.

Goods on display at Service and Trading

Soon, more goods came pouring in; the staff hired to help out in the shop was kept busy recording every item.

Mr. John Lim, a self employed mechanic, decided to join the firm and was given the responsibility to provide service to the outboard motors such as Evenrude and Johnson out boat motors.

As the company expanded, Mr. Lawrence Leong, who was currently employed in Hong Kong and Shanghai bank as a clerk and Mr. Liew Ho Fong, joined the company. Osman the lorry driver, Mr. Pang, a sundry shop sales personnel, also applied to work with the company. Florence Liew and Miss Liew were added to the company's workforce as sales girls. Within a span of several months the company had expanded tremendously. Verities of products ranging from motor vehicles, outboard motors office equipment, home appliances, you name it Service and Trading had it all.

Prior to our company several British companies such as Harrisons and Crosfield, Borneo Company, Boustead, Sime Darby, North Borneo Trading was fully entrenched. Teck Guan and Champion Motors were also dealing with cars. Several Chinese companies had been dealing in timber, plantation, barter trading, sundry goods and other local products. Most were exported to oversea especially Hong Kong and Japan.

This new company called Service and Trading had a daunting task to compete with the well-funded and experience Chinese companies. For me, as a novice in the business world, it was learning on the job experience. Still wet behind the ear, I would be facing a tremendous task ahead of me. We had not built any anchor product that could sustain the company and proper work order of a given time frame. Everything was done in a haphazard manner. This was probably due to their inexperience in the business world. Meanwhile, I had to learn as best as I could, within the work culture of the company. I was not given any specific task, but just to observe and to learn the rules of the game.

There were many guests and customers that came to the shop. One gentleman that often stopped by was Encik Ahmad Daing Mapata, formally came from neighboring countries but had settled in Tawau years ago..

He and several local natives such as Encik Karim, (Fazar township was known as Karim's Pah) NC Dullah Suing, the Kreah family, the Kee family, Kedai Tawakal, the Assah family owned much of the land in town.. I use to see Encik Ahmad Daing Mapata collecting his monthly dues and carrying nothing but a paper bag and walking casually with all the money nicely kept inside. At the end of the day, he would enter the bank and deposit his income without any fuss. After dealing with the bank, his next appointment was with my dad Peter and he would spend some time in the office chitchatting. Eventually, I found out that he had been seeking dad's help to provide him with asthma tablets for his chronic cough. His first house was in the Kampung Ice Box and later built one extra large mansion at Jalan Mawar

Rumah Ahmad Daing Mapata
Tawau Sabah

The mansion of Ahmad Daing Mapata

Encik Ahmad was a philanthropy that donated part of his land at the fringe of the town to the Tawau Mosque committee to erect a mosque which was named Masjid Ahmad Daing Mapata. During the opening, we were all invited to attend the ceremony amongst our Muslim brothers.

*The four of us at Ahmad Daing Mapata Mosque in Tawau: from left, Bryan
Paul Lai, (author) a friend, Patrick Lai and Yusuf Pangiran Abdillah*

Our Tinagat land, the land of my father's dream

*M*y dad Peter had this dream since he left Wallace Bay. A house by the
seaside, free from neighbors and enough elbow areas to move around.. He
had been envisaging it since the day he left Sebatik Island. After months of
intensive search, his quest was answered, when he finally located the ideal
spot at Tinagat beach, that answered his dream.. The land was located right
at the sea front and protected by a big chunk of solid rock.

Our Tinagat Land ,Batu Payung, Tawau 1964

The Tinagat Land that Peter bought, seen just above the beach.

The family was being briefed on the proposal and all of us were brought to the site before making a final decision. I immediately fell in love with the spectacular location. It commanded a panoramic view of Cowie Harbour and Sebatik Island. It covered an area of 4.5 acres, an ideal size to build a cottage and a beautiful garden, with excess land to spare. The decision to purchase the land was unanimous, the family loved it. A month later, the deal was finalized and the purchase price was agreed by both Encik Razala and Dad.

My sister Cabrini enjoys the panoramic view from our Tinagat land, enjoying the scenic view of the sea

Peter Raymond lai admiring the panaromic view of the sea from his dream land Tinagat 1967

My dad Peter admires the view from the land he
bought at Tinagat, Tawau, Sabah.

When the purchase of the land was finalized, our present house at Jalan Kuhara Mile 2 was put up for sale. Dad was so happy in his prize possession. Every afternoon after work, he would drive to the site and took a stroll admiring the land area over and over again. Occasionally, he would sit on the rock and enjoy the sea breeze and the sound of the waves.

One day, Peter was on his usual visit to the area, visualizing the best site to put up the cottage. Out of the blue, a local native by the name of Talip who was staying at the kampong nearby came around. He was an old carpenter and a contractor. It was a pleasant, friendly encounter that turned into a fruitful discourse. Talip, who had years of experience up his sleeves, was confident that he could construct the cottage successfully if given the task. With his assurance, dad agreed to hand over the undertaking of the construction of the house. Throughout the construction, Dad was always present at the site, giving a helping hand and providing the materials required. It took eight months to finish the project.

Evening time at the garden in Tinagat
Petger,Gabriel;a and paul

*Mom Gabriela, Dad Peter and me at the cottage site at Kg
Tinagat, busy trying to beautify the surrounding area.*

My dad Peter building his cottage at Tinagat Hamlet assisted by Encik Talip 1964

*Peter Raymond Lai at the Cottage in Tinagat, actively
involved in the construction of his dream home.*

*O*ur old house at mile 2 Kuhara road was eventually sold. The family moved to Tinagat lock, stock and barrel. Tinagat was around fifteen kilometers away from the town, with no electricity or water provided by the government. We had to use our own generator for electricity and build a big reservoir for stocking up much needed rain water. During drought, we had to ferry water from town.

The lack of water and electrical power did not dampen us living there. The joy of peace, tranquility and fresh air that we relished superseded all other matters. My brother Ambrose and I spent much of our free time sailing our catamaran out to sea or fishing by the kelong (fish-trap sited at sea) nearby that belonged to Mr Koh Bak Chin a fish monger.

My brother Ambrose and I put up the final touch on the catamaran.

The sea beach at the foot of our land in Tinagat. We were preparing to set sail for a fishing trip.

In the afternoon we would set our net by the beach and left it there for several hours. By evening, the net would be full of Ikan Quaci (small fish which are full of bones). Mom and dad would be busy helping us to dislodge the hundreds of fish caught in the net.

The Tinagat Cottage by the sea front, 1966

The Tinagat Cottage by the sea front Tawau Sabah 2007
dream house built by Peter Raymond Lai

Lisa (a relative), Gabriela and Peter in front of the completed house

A touch on the steering wheel.

$\mathcal{I}$n town, at the Service and Trading showroom, several new cars are on display. Lawrence had to move them around as I did not possess any driving license.

Fortunately, my good friend Albert Chong had a car. With his assistance, I was able to begin my first driving lesson and soon, able to manage the cars in the showroom without problems. Those days, anyone who held a valid driving license could tutor any new drivers. The driving test was conducted by the police. I went out with him for a week to improve my driving skill.

At other times, Mr. John Anselmi our director would take me out for a drive in his newly acquired Willies jeep. He would drive around town and gave me some valuable advice on safe driving. With the help of these two gentlemen, I had no problem of passing my driving test.

Dad provided me with an old second hand Triumph car. With Lawrence's help, I modified it into the look of a sports car by getting rid of the roof top, but faced the consequences of not being protected from the weather elements. I had to put up a plastic canvas, each time it rained. What a smart move on my part, an unfortunate inconvenience of having an improvised sports car.

My brother Raphael and Mr Chung, enjoying the open air at our Tinagat Land with my Triumph car.

The company's business thrived and the persons employed were more than enough to handle the everyday running of the enterprise.

I became engrossed in the youth movement and took part in many of its activities, and soon became a committee member.

The keys to the door

*O*n the 29th June of 1964, I was just about to let my birthday pass off without any celebration. In fact, I did not even plan to celebrate it. Mr. John Anselmi and wife Jacky secretly made some preparations to surprise me. They organized a simple party at their residence in Tanjung Batu. I was only told of the party at the last minute and had just enough time to invite several of my close friends. It was a wonderful and enchanted evening of gathering among all my close acquaintances.

At my 21st birthday parfty at Mr John Anselmi residence 1964
Tawau Sabah Malaysia

Suprise party at the house of Mr John Anselmi on the 29 June 1964
At Tanjung Batu Laut, Tawau, Sabah

Some guests relaxing on the patio after a meal at Mr John Anselmi's house. Mr George Yap, the Malayan bank manager, relaxing after a hefty meal.

Games were played during my 21ˢᵗ birthday party

MY CLASS MATE THOMAS KU

*S*everal days after my birthday celebration, by coincidence, I met my best friend from school, Mr. Thomas Ku at the Tawau Sports Club. Due to his work at Sabah Land Development Corporation miles away, he hardly made any trip to town.

We had not seen each other since we left school. We had a wonderful reunion and rekindled memories of our school days. One of our fondest memories was our past stint in Sandakan in the year 1961 when we made a short but unforgettable visit.

Buddies at the Tawau Sport Club having a drinking session
1965 Tawau Sabah Malaysia

Bryan(author) third from the left and Thomas Ku, on my left.

Whilst in Sandakan, we attended a Christmas party organized by the youth movement at the Sandakan Ted Chew Association building. We were invited by Vincent Pang and his sister, Vivian Pang. Another sister by the name of Lucy Pang was not present It was a great crowd amongst the youth of Sandakan and my relatives, such as Joe Mariano, Ricky Azcona, Jimmy Delgado and Regina Delgado. We had a memorable and remarkable evening.

The next day, we left Sandakan and went back to Tawau. I continued to serve in the Youth movement. Mr Philip Yapp became the president, Mr Lee Fah Sing the Vice President, Mr Martin Ho was the secretary and I, an ordinary committee member.

The continuance of life

*M*artin Ho has been a good pal of mine since our school days at Holy Trinity School. We were having our breakfast in front of Harrison and Crosfield when he broke the news that he was getting married to a young beautiful lady named Lo Su Ton. He was searching for a best man for the marriage and had nobody else's in mind except me. I refused to accept his proposal due to my lack of suitable attire for the occasion.

I finally accepted his request after he promised to lend me one of his suits. The night before the wedding, we celebrated Martin's Bachelor Night by watching the film "Ben Hur" at the Empress Theater.

The wedding ceremony was a simple one and it was held at the Chinese Chamber of Commerce. The reception dinner was catered by Pin Fu of the Tawau Hotel.

Those days there were no hotels or restaurants big enough to cater for large functions. The town was just trying to get back to its feet after the great fire of 1953 and subsequent fires that engulfed the shop-houses in town. The Chinese Chamber of Commerce, which was built of permanent structure was the only ideal place to conduct functions or weddings.

The Tawau Chinese Chamber of Commerce

Martin Ho, Lee Fah Sing and I continued our active participation in the youth movement and participated in many of the youth activities. Besides having activities on the Tawau Youth Club's premises, the gathering was also held at a member's house. Many of our youth were at the gathering, including Mr Chong Kon Fui the assistant district officer. It was the evening when cupid struck an arrow into his heart and into the heart of a Miss Ho, and they eventually got married.

Sin On hamlet was formally the domain area for most of the Hakka people. As such, the name Sin On was used by most of the locals and the road was named Sin On. Much of the land belonged to the first inhabitants under the surname of Voo, Lim, Thien, Lee Liew, Loong, Chin and Wong. A hamlet of Hakka population, that in the evening we could see pretty girls washing their clothes along the stream as there were no piped water.. It was also a flood prone area and occasionally crocodiles could be seen when flooded.

The Tawau Youth Club played a very substantial social integration amongst the youth in Tawau. It provided them with some sense of responsibility in the society and had organized many activities for the town people.

Activities of the Tawau Youth Club 1965

*Tawau Youth Activities at Tinagat beach which
provided social integration amongst the races*

Winner of the Walkathon organized by the Tawau Youth Club in 1966

Bicycle race organised by the Tawau Youth Club in 1965
Tawau, Sabah Malaysia

Encik Tahir of JKR, winner of The Bicycle Race,
organized by the Tawau Youth Club in 1966

The winners with the committee of the Tawau Youth Club in 1966

Youth leaders present were Peter Loison, Hassan, Agnes Chow, Theresa Lee, Henry Hiew, Bryan Paul Lai and Suppu Tupi at the Tawau Sports Club.

*Several military personals and the youth of Tawau having
their picnic at the Tinagat Beach in 1965*

*Those present were: Ambrose Lai, Nonez, Raphael Lai, Mr Lim, Daniel,
Cabrini Lai, Gloria Lai, Lee Fah Sing, Helen Orolfo, Veronica Leong, Wong
Nyuk Len, Judy Ng, Bryan Paul Lai(Author). A picnic on the sea front of Helen
Orolfo's house.*

Episode 2

The birth of a nation

*M*alaysia was formed on September 16, 1963. Several former colonies of the British Empire consisted of Malaya, Singapore, Sarawak and Sabah. It was named as Malaysia. Just as the union was underway, Singapore withdrew from the pack after two years, leaving behind Malaya, Sarawak and Sabah.

As the formation was given the green light from Britain, the president of the Republic of Indonesia, Sukarno took a firm stand of going against the union.. He attempted to disrupt the alliance and began to instigate the people of Indonesia to oppose Malaysia. With the spark of a fire, he launched his threat and confronted Malaysia within the same period.

The peaceful scenario that existed after the Second World War in 1945 began to change as the rhetoric of the Indonesian President to attack Malaysia intensified. The populace in this little town of Tawau that has thousand of kilometer border line with Indonesia and just a stone throw from Sungai Nyamuk and Kalabakan knew that confrontation with Indonesia if materialized would cause unforeseen tragedy beyond anyone's imagination. The racial populace of this town, came mainly from neighboring areas and was closely related. The danger of an all out war if happened would bring this town back into the past. There would also be an exodus of people finding safer region in another town. Fortunately, this situation did not materialize..

British air squadron at the Tawau airport providing logistic for the military

The populace was feeling apprehensive, and several had gone overseas to avoid trouble at home. Nevertheless the Malaysian Military and its supporter Britain were quick to respond to address the situation. Tawau suddenly transformed into a Military garrison town. Thousand of military personnel were deployed and a squadron of Britain air power was stationed at the airport.

Our military on sentry duties at the Kalabakan
prefecture Tawau, Sabah, Malaysia 1963-1965

The Malaysian rangers on patrol in Tawau Town in 1963-1965

The built up of the Malaysian Military continued unabated, and the business and daily life of the people were somewhat affected. Some took advantage of providing service and requirements of daily needs to the military personals. No doubt, every nook and corners, especially sensitive areas were closely guarded and security checkpoints were stationed that caused some inconvenience to the people..

The Malaysian Military set up their garrison and camp close to the Government Secondary School, the airport and the Tawau River. Barbed wires and security checkpoints were set up in every strategic area.

*British air squadron personnel relaxing in their tent
at the Tawau Airport, Sabah Malaysia*

To back up the defense of the nation, Britain, as the former colonial power in this region provided the country with the British Air Squadron. They were located adjacent to Kampung Java (local word for village) close to the airport. Datuk Albert Watson the Resident of Tawau had to move out several families affected by the military placement in the Hot Spring area. The airport was busy day and night with military aircrafts plying to and fro, transporting military persons and goods.

British Air force busy bringing in Logistic at the Tawau Airport

For several months the populace of the town watched closely the situation, as they witnessed the arrival of thousands of soldiers with their armored vehicles. They continued their occupation, business and social activities as usual. There were no abnormal happenings that could jeopardize the people's safety.

There were skirmishes along the combat zone of the international boundaries. Beside that, Tawau was in no way affected by the events.. News of daily incidents at the international boundaries was kept under cover, known to security personals only, as the public was not being informed. There were no civilian deaths, direct bombings or destroying of properties. The sound of artery firing could be heard daily, reminding the enemy over the boundaries not to take us for granted. The Malaysian Military was on full alert and capable to thwart any advances by the enemy and to fight off their aggression.

British gunners on standby from any intrusion

Several intrusions was made by the Indonesian military at the Kalabakan prefecture, but were thwarted by the army. Then on the 29 December 1963 under the command of 5 Brigade, one of its units from the 3 RMD was ambushed by the Indonesian Military closest to the Kalabakan River.

The Kalabakan River used by the intruder to attack the military outpost

It was about 30 miles from Tawau and 12 miles from the Indonesian border. Prior to that, the Indonesian unit ransacked a Chinese shop at Surudung laut and plundered all the available goods for their survival. After the brief skirmishes and firepower from both sides came to a standstill, Major Zainal Abidin and seven of his comrades were found dead, and 18 injured. These brave men fought bravely to repel the attackers and managed to foil their advancement. Reinforcement was immediately deployed and several of the intruders were finally tracked, killed and taken in as prisoners.

Aside from the Kalabakan confrontation, an additional incident happened in the heart of Tawau at mile three Kuhara. A lone worker who worked for JKR as handyman for many years was planning to create panic to the populace by poisoning the Tawau water system.,

In all probability, it was due to his patriotic inclination towards his former country that spurred him to act without conscience. If he had succeeded, it could have caused untold damage and great mayhem to the population of Tawau. Fortunately, he was caught by the security guard before he could perform his malevolence..

The first water works amenities in Tawau, built in the
fifties and under the jurisdiction of PWD, that the traitor
tried to sabotage during the confrontation.

The second minor incident occurred in our Tinagat area. My mom Gabriella was in the garden tendering to her flowers. As she was about to turn back to the house, she spotted a boat coming towards the beach. It looked suspicious and she quickly alerted my father, Peter, who was in the house. Thinking that it was better to be safe than sorry, Peter alerted captain Bustami of the Malaysian Engineer. Tungku Osman, commander of the Malaysian army division, immediately dispatched a platoon of snipers and armored vehicle. The intruders were duly arrested. They claimed to be fishermen out on a fishing trip. However, their explanation did not hold any water. They were caught with their pants down as the boat they were travelling in was loaded with weaponry and ammunition. All of them were detained and interrogated by the military intelligence police. This incident was not made known to the public at large.

As a result of the incident, the military took immediate steps in setting up an observation station and machine gun nest at a ridge thirty yards outside of our home just to be on the safe side. Historically, the area was also used by the Japanese military during the Second World War. The Japanese had set up their gun nest on the ridge because of its strategic position, and hundreds of spending cartridges caliber could still be found scattered in the area, remnants of the Second World War in 1941-1945

From that pivot spot and armed with powerful field glasses; the soldiers could track any approaching boats from the direction of the Indonesian territory. They could even spot smoke coming out of the houses of the village of Sungai Nyamuk (Name of a small village at the Indonesian Malaysian border).

The Malaysian Military were well-trained and were fully welcomed by the local population. The daily lives of the populace were not much interrupted and all economic and social activities continued as usual, except some inconveniences of being subjected to searches at security checkpoints located at several strategic locations.

A military vehicle seen right in the middle of the Tawau town,
Sabah, Malaysia, during the 1963-1966 confrontation.

Service and Trading had some dealings with the engineering section of the Malaysian engineering unit and provided spare parts for them. This business transaction resulted in forging a cordial relationship between them and Peter the manager of Service and Trading. As a result, Col. Denger, Major Ah Yong, Captain Bustami and several other officers would visit our family at Tinagat cottage

Helping hand to the community by the Malaysian Military Engineers.

*B*esides protecting the populace, the military provided much needed aid to the local population. They construct road at the Sin On prefecture, building bridges on the Tawau River, and some other areas. A bridge at Hill top was named Tungku Osman Bridge. The engineers were also partly responsible for building the Kalumpang Bailey Bridge that connects Tawau and Semporna. Prior to the bridge being built, the Public Works Department had to use a ferry to go across.

My mom Gabriella at that time was the leading fundraiser for the St Ursula Convent School. With her influence, she managed to persuade the military engineers to prepare the initial ground work for the school. They provided heavy machineries to level the site for the construction of the schoolhouse. This unrecorded gesture and social responsibility by the Malaysian Army helped the fund-raising committee to complete the building of the school according to schedule. Mother John Bosco, the Catholic nun who initiated the building of St Ursula's convent, was grateful for the invaluable assistance of the Malaysian Military Engineers. After much diplomatic fury transpiring among the South East Asian Nation, the confrontation at last ended in the year of 1966 and peace and tranquility were once again restored to the populace of Tawau..

However, beside the soldiers killed in Kalabakan, The military once lost a caribou plane between Sebatik Island and Tawau at the Cowie Bay. Several soldiers were killed. The stretch of sea at the mouth of the Kalabakan river estuary had been known to be treacherous. Throughout the years, several boats plying from Tawau to Nunukan were suddenly hit by waves and unseen menace. Many passengers lost their lives. Experience boatmen would not travel at certain time of the day due to these phenomena.

Salvaging a boat that sunk midway between between Tawau and Sebatik

Rescue team trying to salvage and retrieve the bodies of passengers sunk in Cowie Bay, Tawau Sabah

Photo taken in 1965 at Tawau during the confrontation with Indonesia

Malaysian Military Personals at social functions with the locals in Tawau. Peter Raymond Lai and wife were invited to attend a show at the camp. 1965

*Officers of the Malaysian Military Engineers having
their break at Kem Kukusan Tawau Sabah*

The monument built after the confrontation of
1963–1966 Tawau Sabah next to the Reisent's office

*A memorial was built by the people of Tawau to honor
those killed during the confrontation in 1963-1966*

The Tawau Jaycees international

*J*aycees, an international body, was introduced in Tawau in 1964. It was formed up by several young business entrepreneurs such as Mr. Joseph Lee, Mr. Alex Pang, Mr. David Kah, Mr Terrance Liaw, Mr Henry Lai, Mr Sim Pau Tek, Mr Lee Fah Sing, Mr. Martin Ho and several others. The primary purpose of Jaycees in the community was to infuse the principle of legal philosophy, leadership training and business ethics in a business environment.

Those who had demonstrated excellent leadership ability were accredited as Senator of the Jaycees. I joined the Jaycees in 1965 and in 1966 became one of the board members.

We had several leadership courses and seminars in Kota Kinabalu which I partook. Jaycees Senators in Kota Kinabalu, such as Senator Lim Guan Sing, played an all-important part in promoting the Jaycee movement in Sabah. Tawau Jaycees, with a humble start, had continued to be active and played a major role in Sabah and in particular Tawau. In 1971 two years after I graduated from College, I was again invited to join the Tawau Jaycees. Mr. Charles Leong became the President and I took the post of the secretary for two terms. I left the Jaycee for good in 1973 to concentrate in my profession.

Sabah is trying to stand on its two feet.

*S*abah which had been governed by the British since the Second World War was proceeding gradually in the right course. It was a small state with less than two million populations and was still trying to walk on its two feet. Education was still in a budding state and higher education of the people was still a long way off. Behind the scenario, the British were trying to decolonize areas within their prerogative and forge unity by bringing several colonial states under one umbrella called Malaysia. The Unite Nation was involved and they dispatched a team called the Cobbold Commission to ascertain the wishes of the people. Thus Malaysia was formed and at a later stage Singapore opted out, leaving Malaya, Sarawak and Sabah as an entity of one nation's. As a result the people of Sabah were forced to forge ahead with whoever it had within its means.

Political parties sprung up under ethnic grouping and those who held in power began to make the best of their newly found state of affairs. I was in the midst of this state of affairs, but had no interest to participate. My aims at that time were just the youth movement and had not the faintest idea of going into other field except to search for my bread and butter.

However, I did take part for a while in the formation of an UPKO extended party that was started by Mr Joseph Lee@Libunda for a short stint.

The chairman was Mr Anthony Chan, followed by Mr Richard Lee as the deputy, the secretary, Mr Joseph Mosusa and I took the post as the treasurer and several committee members. This proposal was mooted out by Datuk Donald Stephen. His pursuit was to extend the UPKO party to the Sinos and the Peranakan to form a greater UPKO. Before the green light was approved by the supreme council, Richard took the initiative of forming the protein committee of greater UPKO at Tawau district.

Our activities had to be done at the close door level. The supreme council of UPKO had not given the green light yet. The sole activity that I could recall was an event that the late Datuk Peter Mojuntin instructed us to look into some problem at the Andrassy settlement scheme. Mr. Anthony Chan, Richard Libunda and I rushed to Andrassy during the night to determine what the trouble was. The problem was amicably solved, and before we left, we had a small party

The Andrassy land scheme system was mooted out by the late Datuk Donald Stephen. It was a settlement scheme, which was to provide suitable land for the landless from Kota Kinabalu and its surrounding hamlet. Each participant was given around fifteen to twenty acres of agricultural plot and some financial aid until they could be self-sustaining.

We continued with our normal daily activities and plotted our next step to recruit more members of the Sino communities to participate in the proposed movement. Everything had to be done behind closed doors as the Supreme Executive Council of the UPKO party had not finalized the propose membership. There was no final directive from Kota Kinabalu as we were waiting earnestly for the Supreme Body to sanction our committee.

The local election for the Town Council was approaching, and forms were filled by our proposed party to meet our nominees for the various council posts. Mr. Richard Lee proposed that I stood for the Airfield Ward. I was reluctant, but after thoughtful considerations, accepted his proposal. I referred this matter to our director Mr. John Anselmi for his opinion. He told me to go for it to garner experience. This local election was a legacy handed down by the colonial government during their administrative years. Nevertheless, as the process of candidates from the political party were submitted to the Resident office for action, the regime of the day decided to recant the ongoing requirements and declared that the governing party of the day would appoint their representative to sit in the local council instead. Mr. Herman Luping, the resident administrative officer had to inform all parties affected by this ruling.

This declaration empowered the ruling governing parties to have a total control of the local council at every district. I was relieved by the ruling as it spared me from financial burden. Several weeks later the Chairman, Mr. Anthony Chan, called us for a short meeting and at the gathering solemnly declared that the extended UPKO party had to disband with immediate effect. We were told that a member of the Supreme Council in Kota Kinabalu had objected to the formation of the greater UPKO party. Datuk Donald Stephen had no alternative but to recant his proposal to maintain party's unity. As a result of this declaration, I've lost interest of any political adventure and did not take part in any political party till today..

The birth of Sanya in Tawau

𝒯he formation of Sanya was initiated from Kota Kinabalu by several top guns during the USNO era as commented by Datuk Wilfred Lingham. However, it was Hon Harris Salleh that continued the program and began to implement it throughout the state

Sanya was formed in Tawau on 5 September 1966. The Hon Encik Harris Salleh the Protem President of Sanya Sabah, Encik Jack Chin and Encik Dirius Damile visited Tawau to explain in three languages the purpose of the formation of Sanya. Around fifty Tawau youths took part in the dialogue held at the Tawau Sports Club. Encik Robert Cheng, the chief of the information department, unofficially chaired the meeting. He gave a brief welcoming speech to all the guests and youths in attendance.

Among those present were N. C. Tintingan who spoke about the purpose of the Sanya Youth movement. Encik Kassim Kamidin then proposed that a protein committee be formed in Tawau headed by Mr. Philip Yapp. He was seconded by O. T. Abdul Rahman. Mr. Philip Yapp due to his imminent transfer to Kota Kinabalu declined the offer and instead proposed Mr. Robert Cheng to lead the Tawau Branch. He accepted the proposal and the nomination were closed. O.T Abdul Rahman was proposed by Hon Harris Salleh as the deputy president. He was seconded by Encik Kassim Kamidin and elected.

Mr. Ajaib Singh declined the post of secretary, so it went to O. T. Abdul Rahman as Proposed by Hon Encik Harris and seconded by Encik Kassim Kamidin.

Hon Treasurer, Encik Bryan Paul Lai declined nomination as he was about to leave for Kota Kinabalu. Mr. Ajaib Singh than proposed Encik Lim Piang Kong. Encik Philip Yapp seconded the proposal and Mr Lim Piang Kong became the treasurer. There were five committee members. Encih Paidin, Cik Theresa Lee, Encik Yahya, Encik Mohd Sa'ad and Encik Santani. With the formation of Sanya as the youth body in Tawau, the Tawau Youth Club, which had been active since 1962 began to lose its significance as many dedicated past youth leaders left the district. The Tawau Youth Club Building was gradually taken over by Sanya and later, by the Ministry of Youth.

The Tawau Youth Club built in 1964
by the effort of Tawau Youths under the
leadership of Mr Philip Yapp

The Tawau Youth Club building built by the youths of Tawau in 1964
under the leadership of Mr Philip Yapp who was the President of the club.
Now it's been taken over by the ministry of youth as their official office.

SABAH NATIONAL YOUTH ASSOCIATION
TAWAU BRANCH

MINUTES OF THE MEETING OF THE PROVISIONAL SANYA, TAWAU BRANCH HELD
AT THE TAWAU SPORTS CLUB PREMISES AT 5.30 P.M. ON 5TH SEPT., 1966.

Present : 50 people from the different races, including N.C. Titingan,
Enche Kassim Kamidin and other prominent people in Tawau.

Before the meeting, Enche Robert Cheng gave an introduction
of the meeting. Then Enche Philip Yap was proposed by Enche Ajaib
Singh Maan to be the recorder for the meeting. He was also seconded
by N.C. Titingan.

The meeting was addressed by: 1) Hon. Enche Harris, Pro-tem
President of SANYA, in
English and National Language.

                      ii) Enche Jack Chin in Chinese, and

                      iii) Enche Dirius Banil in Kadazan.

N.C. Titingan was also invited to give his opinion to the
attendance regarding the formation of the SANYA in Tawau.

After a lengthy discussion, Enche Kassim Kamidin proposed
to form a pro-tem committee to finalise matters with regards to
SANYA, Tawau Branch. This decision was seconded by O.T. Abd. Rahman.

The following were nominated to serve in the pro-tem Committee:-

1. Branch Leader - 1. Enche Philip Yap was proposed but he
declined nomination as he is expecting
to have a transfer shortly.
2. Enche Robert Cheng was then proposed
by Enche P. Yap, seconded by Enche
Kassim Kamidin.
Enche Robert Cheng was elected.

2. Deputy Branch Leader - O.T. Abd. Rahman was proposed
by Hon. Enche Harris, seconded
by Enche Kassim Kamidin. Elected.

3. Secretary - 1. Enche Ajaib Singh declined nomination.
2. Enche Ibrahim was proposed by Hon.
Enche Harris, seconded by Enche
Kassim Kamidin. Elected.

4. Treasurer - 1. Enche Paul Lai declined nomination.
2. Enche Lim Piang Kong was proposed
by Enche Ajaib, seconded by Enche P.
Yap. Elected.

5. Committee Members: 1. Enche Paidin
2. Che Teresa Lee
3. Enche Santani
4. Enche Yahya
5. Enche Mohd. Sa'ad.

N.C. Titingan has kindly consented to donate $50.- towards
the expenditure of the Provisional SANYA, Tawau Branch.

As there was no other business the Branch Leader, Enche Robert
Cheng closed the meeting at 7 p.m.

Tawau: 5th Sept., 1966.

(Philip Yap)
Recorder for the Meeting.

The above minute depicted the formation of Sanya in Tawau in 1966

Episode 3

The Tawau Youth Movement

$\mathcal{T}$he Tawau Youth movement was meted out in the year 1962. It provided a groundbreaking opportunity for the thousands of youths currently living in Tawau to channel their talents and energy into something positive. It was also a chance for the young population to serve the society.

This decision and vision was meted out by a conscientious gentleman Mr Raymond Pritchard. He answered the silent call from the voice of the youth, the young men and women of this vibrant town of Tawau.

It was in the year of 1962 when Mr. Raymond Pritchard, a District Officer by profession presented his idea to a group of conscientious citizens of the town. His proposal was keenly accepted by the local influential leaders of Tawau. He galvanized the youth and teachers from the local schools to attend a consequential gathering to get their personal views. He was encouraged by their positive response and immediately took steps to outline the first Youth movement called the Tawau Youth Club.

The initial launch was carried out at the Tawau Chinese Chamber of Commerce. There were more than sixty youths attending the event. The bulk of them came from schools in Tawau accompanied by several conscientious teachers such as Mr David Kah, Mr Thomas Tan, Miss Alice Kim, Mr Jimmy Cheah and several others. Local high profiled leaders who were present were HC Abu Bakar Tintingan, Mr William Thien, Mr Philip Yapp, Mr George Yapp, Mr Pang Su Lam, Mr Lim Piang Kong and the Local Education officer. This close-knitted youth populace was suddenly given an opportunity to contribute to nation building which had been an oversight since the end of the second world war of 1945.

The rules and bylaws of the club were formulated and registered with the registrar of societies. Election of committees was duly held and it was done at an utmost democratic way and votes were counted with an official observing at every count. It was indeed a good beginning, for the youths to emulate the democratic principle of the nation that could play a long lasting avenue for this young country of Sabah.

Members of the youth on duty counting the votes for the official office bearers of the club in 1962 from left: Beatrice Hee, Annie Hee, Mary Lu and several other youths

During the Chinese New Year, a social gathering was organized by the committee at the top floor of the Chinese Chamber of Commerce.

More than a hundred youths attended that event. An impromptu singing contest was held. At first, all the members were reserved and too shy to participate in the contest. Suddenly, I was pushed up the stage by my friend Martin Ho. I felt shy at first, but decided to be sporting and took part of the fun of it. I sang an old song entitled "I am Just a Lonely Boy" by Paul Anka.

I must have broken the ice, for after that, more youths braced themselves by going up the stage to sing. It was a wonderful moment.

After the contest, I was surprised to be judged the winner and was awarded a photo album. The ladies section was won by a Miss Chin Sui Jing.

As the evening continued, the crowd began to be more at ease and many took part in the various activities planned for the night. It was the first time that the Youth of Tawau were able to interact with one another in such a cordial and friendly atmosphere. Many had a wonderful evening as laughter filled the air and all the guests enjoyed the goodies, cakes and drinks provided.

I continued being in the association, but just as a member and not actively involved in their functions or meetings. Nonetheless, my degree of involvement took a drastic change when I received a call from an old acquaintance by the name of Miss Alice Kim.

Miss Alice and her family lived close to the Tawau River, just after the Tawau Bridge at Jalan Kuhara. I was well acquainted with the folks. I have known them since the days when I was just a little boy staying in the boarding house at Holy Trinity. Her mother, a soft spoken woman, had been most helpful to me with my laundry. Alice was currently teaching at Holy Trinity Primary School, as well as actively involved in the youth association

The youth actively involved in gatherings to foster friendship. Depicted in the pictures were From left: Theresa Yapp, Anthony Nair, Maria Nair, the Phan sisters, Glen Quienliven, Mary Chow, Agnes Chow, George Loong, Bernard Loong, Bryan Paul Lai, Cabrini Lai, Albert Chong and several others

Some of the Tawau Youth at the Youth club function: Those present were Peter Wong, Chan, George Chang, Chung and several others

That one call, made to me completely changed my perspective on the youth movement. She presented a brief account of the club and gave me the opportunity to be involved and served on her committee which she currently hold. After giving some thoughts, I accepted her offer and began to show some interest in her work. She was the chairlady for the social sub-committee. I participated in many of her meetings and events. As the months passed by, I began to take a more active role in most of the youth functions. It encouraged and built my enthusiasm in the movement and spurred me to be more responsive to the youth cause..

The youth of Tawau at one of the functions. From left Bryan Paul Lai, Francis Chan, Cabrini Lai, George Chang, Chung and Ambrose Lai

Members of the Tawau Youth Club having their picnic at the Tinagat Beach

Mr. Raymond Pritchard, the outstanding gentleman who provided staunch guidance, was the forefront of all the activities.. He put in every effort to promote the youth movement, to ensure that the activities moved on the right track. Beside the Tawau Youth movement, he took great effort to promote the Boy Scout activities at Holy Trinity Secondary School. It was indeed a great success as many of the students took part in the scouting activities.

The youths of the Holy Trinity scouting fraternity inspired by Mr Raymond Pritchard. Those present were: Martin Liang, Michael Lutam, Glen Quienliven, Richard Primus, Francis Anthony, Andrew Thien, James Ku, Thomas Chang Kin Hing, Kamil Kassim Kamidin, Daniel Lai, Hassan, Matthew Anthony, Peter Loong, Jeoffrey Tan, Booth will, Arnesto F. Irine Maluda and the rest of the gang

Several years later, he was called to Kota Kinabalu to hold an important post and left Tawau for good. His legacy to the youth movement was greatly appreciated by the Tawau Youths.. I am sure very few of the new generation knew of the effort put in by Mr Raymond Pritchard and his predecessor.

His position was taken over by another proactive gentleman who had been a most well-known person in the banking sector. Mr Philip Yapp had been the manager for several years at Malayan Bank and had always participated in the movement since it was initiated by Mr. Raymond Pritchard. With his leadership and dedication, he started to instigate the formation of a building fund committee.

A sub-committee for the building fund was subsequently set up.

Several meetings were held to finalize the program of raising the required amount and the type of building suitable at that juncture. It was then decided to raise funds by holding a fun-fair during the Chinese New Year. It was a time when the Chinese populace would be in the mood of departing with their hard-earned money to a worthy cause.

It was to be held in front of the old Town Board office, known as the Rest House during the colonial days. We galvanized all the members to participate in the project and finally, at the end of the day, were able to raise a sum of around more than thirty thousand dollars.

Mr. Philip Yapp had done a tremendous job and was able to witness his effort in the construction of the building at Jalan Utara before he left for Kota Kinabalu. The building cost was more than the sum obtained. It was in the red for several thousands of dollars. Fortunately, Mr Yapp Man Siau, the town board executive officer, kindly provided the club the extra sum to cover up the deficit. The loan was settled within a year.

The Tawau Youth club building built in the year 1964
that stood at Jalan Utara till today 2015

Mr. Fung Cheong Ming, the Tawau Education Officer who had the youth movement close to his heart became the advisor to the club until he was transferred back to Kota Kinabalu. Consequently, another government officer by the name of Herman Luping, attached to the Resident Office, continued to become the club's third advisor. The club continued to progress successfully, due to the dedication shown by those gentlemen concerned.

With the new building, the youths in Tawau were finally able to conduct their weekly activities. With the exemplary leadership of the youth, many activities were held successfully, such as The Bicycle race, Mr. Tawau contest, Walkathon and other social activities organized by the club. Picnics at Tinagat Beach were occasionally held, giving an opportunity for the various races of youths in Tawau to bond.

The Tawau Youth Club Organising the Mr Tawau contest 1965

The Mr Tawau Contest organized by the Tawau Youth Club. Mr Herman Luping the youth advisor was beside me watching the contestants in the background. Mr Herman Luping was subsequently transferred to Kota Kinabalu and became the Attorney General of Sabah.

*Members of the Tawau Youth Movement taking
a break at Tinagat Beach, Tawau*

Youth at the picnic ground on Tinagat beach. Portrayed in the picture is Azis Assah, sharing a joke with Henry Hiew, Chong Kon Fui, Sandra Braganza, Moin and several others. The melting pot of various ethnic group of Tawau.

The youth movement subsequently was formed in several towns in Sabah such as Kota Kinabalu, Sandakan, Papar, Labuan and Tawau. This movement became an affiliated body called SAYC or Sabah Association of Youth Clubs. Seminars were then held at respective towns. These seminars were participated by youth throughout Sabah. The first seminar was held in Kota Kinabalu, in 1963 headed by Mr Philip Yapp and others, followed by Tawau in 1964.

Papar Seminar

The seminar at Papar was officiated by his Excellency the Yang DI-Pertua Negara Datuk Pangiran Hj Ahmad Rafaee. The MAYC or Malaysian Association Of Youth Club from West Malaysia sent one representative as an observer. The speakers during the seminar were as follows: Hon Minister for Natural Resources Encik Thomas Jayasuria and Datuk Donald Stephen, the Honorable Chief Minister of Sabah. They spoke on the roles of youth in state building, especially as Sabah was just a young state at that time.

At this seminar, Yapp Pak Leong was elected as the first President, to lead the association of SAYC in Sabah and Martin Ho as the deputy President for Tawau region. It was a very successful seminar and Tawau was accredited as one of the most active youth associations in Sabah. It had successfully organized several events such as the body building competition, The Walkathon, the Bicycle Race, and even Bahasa Malaysia classes for those who were interested to participate.

Other activities carried out were social activities such as picnics to foster better integration amongst the youth of the various races. We also have social functions called jam session which was held at the club premises on every Saturday afternoon.

The youths at the Sandakan airport- Mary Lu of Tawau, Maria Nobleza, Marvel Nobleza and several officials of the Sandakan Youth, waiting for the arrival of Datuk Koo Siak Chu to officiate the youth seminar

The chairman of the Sandakan Youth Club Mr Marvel Nobleza
welcoming the Hon Minister Datuk Koo Siak Chu and introduced him
to the youth representatives from the various youth clubs in Sabah

*a*fter Sabah gained its independence and joined Sarawak and Malaya
to form Malaysia, it was the policy of the federal government through the
ministry of youth to bring all the ethnic youths in the country together.
Sabah was allocated to submit three names and Sarawak seven. I felt
very honored when I was among the three to be nominated to represent
Sabah. Encik Jafar Lasim and other youth from Papar were the other two
representatives. We were brought to Pertake Kuala Kubu Baharu in the
State of Selangor.

The national youth training center at Pertake Kuala Kubu Baharu Selangor.
Sabah Representative: Encik Jafar Lasim, Bryan
Paul Lai and a youth from Papar.

The one-month youth training program was fully sponsored by the Ministry of Youth, under the Sabah State Government. The said seminar provided the youth of Malaysia ample opportunity to understand the concept of nation building by the youth of today. My active involvement in the youth body gave me the opportunity to understand the quest that we had to undertake for a just and peaceful coexistence among the various ethnic groups in this country.

The training session lasted for several weeks. Besides our group, members of the national sports body were also having their training session at the same location.

I was surprised to meet an old acquaintance, Mr. Albert Chong, my school day's sports opponent in the high jump competition. Albert had been a good pal of mine and was kind enough to teach me to drive in his fiat car. Because of his vast experience in sports, he was nominated by the Sabah Sports Council to attend the course.

The youth training lasted for several weeks at the youth training Centre. It gave us a perspective view of the various youth organizations in the country. In the State of Sabah, the youth organization encompassed all the various races and ethnic diversity, whereas in West Malaysia the Youth organization that I've visited was mostly based on racial domain. This made me feel proud of our youth organization indeed!

Berjumpa dengan orang Sabah yang berkhidmat dan berlatih di kem tentera Tanjung Malim.
Lt Karim Ghani dari Kota Kinabalu,Khamis dari Tawa dan seorang Lt dari Kota Kinabalu.

During our course, the three of us from Sabah, Encik Jafar Lasim,
Papar Youth and I paid a brief visit to our Sabahan military personnel
undergoing training at Tanjung Malim, Kuala Lumpur, Malaysia.

During the course in Pertake, we were given a tour of Kuala Lumpur and the opportunity to visit the First Prime Minister of Malaysia Tungku Abdul Rahman at his residence.

Youth at the resident of Tungku Abdul Rahman,
the first Prime Minister of Malaysia.

Tungku Abdul Rahman shares a joke with the
participants. The author is in a black suit.

At the residence of Tungku Abdual Rahman, the first Prime Minister of Malaysia 1965. Bryan (the author) is as far right.

Ungku Moksin introducing the participants to the first Prime Minister of Malaysia, Tungku Abdul Rahman.

Tungku Abdul Rahman at ease talking to the participant
from Sarawak while Ungku Moksin looked on.

Finally, as the seminar ended, we were given the opportunity to visit the various youth organizations in several East Coast States..

It was a wonderful holiday experience, fully sponsored by the Ministry of Youth. Our journey began in Kuala Lumpur by train and was accompanied by officials from the youth ministry. Our first destination was Penang. We stayed two nights, and left Kedah the next morning by bus The next day, we travelled to Terangganu, Kelantan and Perlis. Our journey took us ten days before finally returning to Sabah.

Back to Tawau, I was fully engrossed in the youth movement We continued to organize youth activities that could entice and encouraged the young people of Tawau to be a member of the youth movement. We created awareness amongst the youth to partake in the organization. The youths were given the opportunity to acquire certain organizing skills and the know-how to explore their hidden talents and potential.

We travelled to Semporna and other districts to get young adults to organize themselves as a youth body.

Front from left: Miss Theresa Yapp, Miss Mary Lu, Miss Annie Hee
Behind: Peter Loison, Bryan and two others.

Front from left: Roland Gomes, Constance Gomes, Beatrice Hee, Annie Hee Behind Bryan Paul Lai (Author)

Bryan P. Lai, Martin Ho and Lee Fah Sing (not in picture) on board the ship to Semporna to activate the youth movement in the town

We visited Semporna to galvanize the youth to form their
youth association in 1965. Mr Ispal of Semporna was
temporarily appointed as the proposed youth leader.

The three of us from the Tawau Youth Club travelled to Semporna by steamship. We met Encik Ispal and a teacher from SMK Semporna. Encik Ispal was an old acquaintance of mine from Holy Trinity School in Tawau. We travelled to Semporna by steamship as there was no road overland. The sea was not deep enough to warrant a jetty so the ship had to anchor further from the shoreline.

Suddenly, out of the blue, came these little canoes manned by little indigenous kids, ranging from as young as five to fifteen years of age, paddling to the side of the ship with their little canoes oblivious of the danger. They then started putting up their hands asking for drinks and money. Many of the passengers threw coins and bottle drinks to the kids and they would dive into the sea to retrieve the coins and other goods from the seabed.

When all the passengers disembarked and goods destine for Semporna unloaded onto the smaller vessel, their ship would immediately set sail back to other ports. We spent several days in Semporna trying to activate the youth movement. Our mission completed, we left for Tawau on the next steamship. Encik Ispal was given the responsibility to continue with the proposed movement.

Meanwhile, another scenario cropped up in the year 1965. The Hon. Encik Harris Salleh proposed the formation of Sanya. Hon. Encik Harris made a short trip to Tawau to clarify his proposal to the Tawau Youth movement. The Tawau Youth Committee met him at the restaurant of Tawau Hotel and was provided with a simple lunch.

The proposition was well received by the Tawau Youth Club Committee and took note the concept behind the establishment, as explicated by the Hon Encik Harris Salleh. The Tawau Youth committee, however, did not commit itself immediately, as it required consultation with the Sabah Youth Body before any decision could be reached. It was only in 1966 that Hon. Encik Harris brought his high powered delegates from Kota Kinabalu, as I had mentioned in my previous chapter and immediately formed Sanya in Tawau which was headed by Robert Cheng.

In 1966, Mr Lee Fah Sing became the President of the Tawau Youth Club. Mr Philip Yapp the former President did not stand for any election as he was to be transferred to Kota Kinabalu to take up his new appointment. Mr. Martin Ho became the deputy president and I took the post of the secretary.

When Mr Lee Fah Sing was promoted by the bank as the manager of the HSBC branch in Papar, Martin Ho took over as the President and I became the deputy President. By the end of the year, though, I had to resign from the youth movement as I had to report to college in January 1967. With many of its pioneering leaders gone, the Youth Club continued to function till 1969 when it was absorbed into the Sanya movement. The youth club building was fully utilized by the ministry of youth at their main center for youth activities.

The Tawau Youth Club, which played an important integral part of the Tawau Youth Movement and had been the pride of the youth in the sixties had now been left with an uncertain future and gradually disappeared through a natural death in the year 1970.

The year from 1964 to 1966 had been the year of culminating friends from all walks of life. Albert Chong, Moen and several others had been my regular buddy. Both Albert Chong and Moen were my schoolmate and throughout the years were actively involved in the school sports. Albert was employed by Borneo Abaca as a trainee officer. Our favorite spots of rendezvous were the BAL executive club. The club had been their week end sanctuary to meet friends for a party or drinks. It was normal for the senior executive such as Mr Dixon Chok to organize barbeque at his resident to dissipate tension and boredom by having small gatherings at home amongst close friends.

Meanwhile, Service and Trading continued to function well with all its acquired agency and goods. I continued to learn as mush as possible the art of the trade while on the job. It was not an easy task as the company had not formulated any work order, or had any fix clientele to distribute the goods that we dealt with, in spite of the many products that we hold, such as National and Ecko radio, Gestener, ICI products, Simca, Willys Zeep, Mercedes Benz and outboard motors

The company had also acquired insurance agencies and continued to promote their products to the general public. The car business was the most challenging that we ever had to handle. Lawrence Leong had been appointed in the vehicle and spare parts department. Mr. John Lim, the outboard section and Mr Liew Ho Fong and Mr. Pang as the general salesman for the other products and agencies. Ah Sung or Mr. Lee happened to be the first customer to purchase a Mercedes Benz and converted it into a taxi in the Tawau district.

Service and Trading did reasonably well for several years, but luck began to change in the year 1968 when it diverted into the timber business in

Indonesia. Mr George Chin and Mr Lee were part of the group from Tawau that had an interest in the new project.

The company began to lose its momentum and no senior person in the company was able to manage the running of the business effectively. Peter spent the bulk of his time travelling to Indonesia and John Anselmi to his plantation. As a consequence, Service and Trading lost its momentum and finally had no other choice but to pass all the agencies to other companies. I left the company and entered Gaya College to peruse my own destiny.

Episode 4

Daunting task of a business endeavor

From Left: John Anselmi, Peter Lai and a an
acquaintance from the Armed Forces
Stationed in Tawau in 1965

*M*y dad Peter Raymond Lai and his associate Mr. John Anselmi had embarked into a business enterprise. A venture called Service and Trading that began in 1962, before Malaysia was formed. It was their quest, to enter into unchartered field, on the anticipation that business would improve with the new scenario.

74

Business activities took a big leap ahead as additional individuals were added to the company to provide for the expanding enterprise. When Malaysia was formed and the confrontation began, the company Service and Trading which had predicted the case managed to intercept some of the business activities.

Peter and John Anselmi was both novice in the business universe. Peter, a medical hospital assistance by profession and John, a planter. It was their mission to embark into commerce, and if doing well, would make them well-off.

Business contacts throughout the world were made, such as from West Malaysia, Singapore, Australia and others. The representatives of these companies came in droves to introduce their products to penetrate the Tawau market.

Mr. John Anselmi, took a short trip to Singapore, and was enticed to order varieties of merchandise to be marketed in this little town without much deliberation or consultation from his partner Peter. It was indeed a daunting project to market high end goods to the low end populace.

Service and Trading were offered to be the sole agent for various heavy duty merchandise such as Mercedes Benz, Simca, Mitsubishi, ICI, Outboard Motors, National Radios, Ecko, Foremost Milk, Gestener machines and many others. Insurance agencies were also appended to the list of the business carried out by Service and Trading. You name it, Service and Trading had it.

With a small workforce of eight to ten persons, the team was more than plenty to handle the study load, but its basic infrastructure of giving service to customers was far from sufficient.

Bryan at the Agricultural Road show 1964

*Service and Trading putting up a display at
the Agricultural Station in Tawau*

Pre Independence

*P*rior to Sabah's independence, several well-known British companies had entrenched itself into a number of business enterprises in the country. They were dealing with timbers, trading commodities and home necessities. They offered much needed jobs for the locals. Much of the income derived was reimbursed back to their shareholders and Sabah did not make a great deal in terms of reinvestment.

When Sabah gained its autonomy, and later shown as a liberal nation, it joined the other independent state of Malaya, Sarawak and Singapore that created a new country called Malaysia. Singapore opted out of the federation after some irreconcilable disagreements. Sarawak and Sabah remained. Several political parties surfaced to the fore and with the high potential of the resources available and the realization of its leaders, enmity between the parties began to surface. An alliance was made on ethnic ground by parties to champion and strengthen their hold.

As political leaders began to exploit for influence, many started to comprehend the vast potential of the State Natural Resources. This immature, unprepared state that was still relishing from the destruction of the Second World War was suddenly being persuaded by its Colonial Britain to proclaim its independence..

The populace during the last census was only under two million and the educational standard of its people was far from being able to fend for itself. Even so, North Borneo had no choice but to take the verdict even though its population was still learning to walk.

Newly minted politician began to shove their ways to gain political mileage and belligerent in seat allocation in the power structure of the ruling party. External influence from another entity was the norm of the day as the people of Sabah looked on feeling marginalized.

My sister Cabrini fell in love and wedded a man named Ahmad Yussuf. My brother in law was attached to the Marine Department Tawau.. However, seeing the opportunity, he left his job and joined one of the governing political parties. He sustained a tight rapport with Datuk Hamid, the son of Tun Mustapha. They became close comrades and took part in many of the political party events.

Encik Ahmad Yussuf

At one of the general elections held in the State, Encik Ahmad Yussuf was nominated to represent USNO for the Tawau constituency. Unluckily for him, he did not galvanize enough support from the town folks. He lost both to Hiew Min Kong of Berjaya and Michael Lim of PBS. Ahmad Yusuf was further disappointed when Datuk Hamid bin Tun Mustapha, his mentor's political career did not live long enough for him to be able to fully commit to the party's struggles. Datuk Hamid succumb to his illness and untimely passed away.

Encik Ahmad Yussuf, who had been earmarked by Tun Mustapha to oversee his proposed restaurant in London, had to abandon the plan. It was an unforeseen tragedy that impeded his political career.

In spite of this uncertainty, Encik Ahmad Yussuf continued to struggle for the party and still had some remnants of support from his old colleague for the next few years. Nevertheless, with new political parties mushrooming like nobody's business, the dynamic scenario of the racial composition changed as the years passed, Ahmad Yussuf had no option but to set low and gradually, left the political scenery.

Demand for natural resources.

*C*ommodities such as timber were sought throughout the world and their prices took an upward trend.

The demand created an outburst of thousands of virgin forest in Sabah being exploited to the fullest, and those in the cradle of power had full advantage of the situation.

Temporary jungle tracks and roads were built right into the heart of the forest to gain access to the lucrative commodities. Areas in Tawau such as Sin On Tiku, Kalabakan, Luasung, Brumas, Wallace Bay, Tingkaya, Bena, Balung and most areas in Tawau, Lahad Datu, Semporna, Kunak and other portions of the State of virgin forest were subjugated without restriction, except for first class forest reserves or water catchment areas.

The sought after timbers, and road accessibility in the heart of the jungle had created another playground for wildlife hunters. It was a hunting paradise for them as the plentiful of wild beasts that had existed peacefully for thousands of years were finding it hard to defend themselves from the onslaught of poachers and hunters. These once timid and docile wild animals, hitherto unaware of some other creature called 'man', began to learn to avoid their adversary by hiding deep in the inaccessible jungle..

Round timbers in Wallace Bay ready for export

Some hunters took it as a weekend getaway while others exploited it as an economic initiative. Both activities took its toll to the wildlife population. The wildlife department was caught off guard, and hastily upgraded themselves to deal with the issue. Well known wildlife such as rhinos, Orang Utan, Proboscis monkeys, elephants, Honey Bear, and other exotic creatures and plants were in danger of being wiped out from the state forest.

However, the government of the day had to be commended for its efforts to build thousands of low cost housing for the lower income group in the seventies, following the housing developers that accelerated the housing industries in Tawau.

This pace of development coincided with the development of Service and Trading, as the timber fever was still milling around above the clouds and the management of Service and Trading was not exempted from thinking big.

This company was offered a timber concession in Bogor Samarinda, Indonesia that covered several hundred thousand of acres. Not wanting to miss the opportunity of the lucrative timber business, they accepted the offer and formed a syndicate of three entities, comprising the Service and Trading, a Japanese company and Colonel Samsie of Indonesia.

*Peter Raymond Lai my dad, with two of his Japanese
Associates in Bohor Samarinda Indonesia, 1970.*

As agreed in the memorandum, the Japanese company would provide the financial outlay, Service and Trading the operation and the Indonesian partner the local administration and dealing with the Indonesian Government. It took several months before the operation began its full swing..

As this new enterprise started to move forward, business at Service and Trading began to lose its impetus. Peter my dad travelled to Indonesia every month with our cabin cruiser 'Flipper' powered by two 80 horsepower direct to Tarakan bypassing Nunukan. The main focus of Service and Trading was the timber enterprise. As a result, with no one to manage into the core business of Service and Trading, the company gradually looses its momentum.

I had no experience running this company as I was not fully trained in the daily running of the enterprise and had no basic foundation in the business world. This unexpected unsettled situation gave me second thoughts about remaining on board. I also realized that I was not cut out to be a businessman and decided to move on with my own plan before the whole matter collapsed onto my shoulder. I was determined to search for my dream and future prospect on my own. With regret, I left the company.

Finding the true path of destiny.

*M*y brother Daniel came home from Gaya College for a month's vacation. He had earlier enrolled into this college, as he intended to pursue a career in teaching.

During one of our conversations at tea time, he provided me with some constructive and useful information about life in college. I was intrigued by his disclosure and after seriously contemplating about it for several days; I decided to make a go for a teaching career too.

After getting some information from friends, I found out that Mr. Benjamin Kouju was currently attached at Gaya College as a lecturer. He was my old pal during those years in the Youth Movement and a very close acquaintance.

Without any qualms, I gave him a call and inquire about the admission requirements. I was surprised when he ordered me to attend college immediately, without any formal application. He listed my name in the admission list and told me to report to the college soonest possible. Daniel my brother was happy when he found out that I was accepted and would be with him in college. Thus began my teaching career.

Those days teachers were in short supply and as a young country, it was paramount that the populace had to be educated at all cost. Many were sent overseas to equip themselves in every field available. Many schools were built and required a teaching force that could educate the populace at a short period of time.

Teachers training colleges provided free admission. A travel grant and a monthly allowance were also given to each participant. There were many applicants from Tawau, and we were all given the same flight booked by the Education Department. We travelled by Sabah Airways on a plane called Dakota from the old Tawau Airport, which has since been renovated to cater for the ever increasing air travelers.

The teacher trainees at the airport waiting to travel by air to Kota Kinabalu
From left: Ku Ting Chai, Helen Chia, Regina Liew, Lily
Chia, Lilian Koh, Bryan Paul Lai (Author) Chung Vui Tung,
Riduan Donald, Daniel Lai and another trainee.

We arrived in Kota Kinabalu. My brother and I took a taxi to the college. I was given a room shared by five others. The following day after the registration, all of us were required to sit for a trial test. The outcome of the test would decide which class we would be allocated to.

The following day we went into the class with our names listed on the door. The trainees were placed in classes called P1, P2 and P3 or S1 and S2. I was placed in P3. There were around thirty of us in this group, from all walks of life and from different towns. Most came as far as Kudat, Kota Belud, Ranau, Sandakan, Tenom, Keningau, Penampang, Papar, Labuan, Tawau and even from West Malaysia.

Ice-breaking Session in the Gaya College Hall

Our class in 1967 at Gaya College Kota Kinabalu

Standing from left top: *Mr. Vasikaran, Mr. Aziz Assah, Mr. Range Morris, Mr. George Goh, Mr Richard* and *Mr Victor Yen*

Standing second row: *Mr Linus Tokujup, Mr Jimmy Lee, Mr Baljit Singh, Mr Mujiman, Mr Wee San Phin, Mr Abdul Rahman* and *Mr Gulam.*

Sitting from left: *Miss Mariam, Pauline Shim, Miss Ignesia Lee, Miss Lilian Koh Lee Kyaw, Mr. Bryan Paul Lai, Miss Jessica Tinus, Miss Rose Wong, Miss Regina Liew, Miss Linda Mardawan* and *Miss Cathey Wong.*

During our first get-together in the class, most of us were able to get along with one another and the ice was broken instantly. I was selected as the temporary class prefect to handle class matters and as a conduit between the administration, the staff and the teacher trainees. The final class election was held a month later and the class unanimously reelected me as their representative.

Settling down comfortably in college, I finally felt a sense of relief, knowing that this was what I wanted to do, and where I wanted to be. It was a huge relief to be able to see a light at the end of the tunnel.

The college environment gave us some sense of self confidence in life and it was well-run by the college authorities, led by Mr. Tod from United Kingdom, and assisted by another lecturer from the same country. I was confident that I would be able to deal with and to finish the training without much fuss. My involvement in business and association for the last two years had given me ample grass root experience in dealing with associations, human nature and an insight into the business world. It was a short stint, but enough for me to realize that I was not cut into the business world.

Students at Gaya College having fun with their history project 1968

The lively jokers doing a history project: Agnesia Lee, Baljit Singh, Robert Vitalis, Abdul Rahman, Range Morris, Azis Assah Standing: *Ku Ting Chai, Mujiman, Gulam, Jaidin, Jimmy Lee*

A week later, another student came from Tawau. As the class prefect, I welcomed her and gave her all the help she required.

Besides focusing on our academic performance and methodology of teaching, we were required to take part in sports and other activities such as the scout movement, photography, music and other areas of outdoor activities.

In the past, ever since I was just a little boy, my life had been mostly centered in scouting activities. It was quite natural that my interest and focus would be the scout movement. The lecturer in charge of this movement was our BM lecturer Cikgu Jikal. After being with him for several months in the Scouting activities, he was offered a chance to study abroad. He turned over the responsibilities to me and told me to take charge of the movement.

Gaya Collegian sports team at Kent College field Tuaran
1968 Kota kinabalu

*Gaya College Sports Contigent at the Inter-college Sports
meet at the Kent College sports field, Tuaran, Sabah.*

I was reluctant to accept the responsibility, as my credential was not up to par with the movement's requirement. My friend Normatusin from Papar who was currently holding a wood badge, beseeched me to take the job. That, and all the coaxing and support from the other scouters, I finally accepted the offer.

Recollections for some of the scouters that I could trace are as follows:

By merit of my position as the scoutmaster from a teachers training college, I was invited to attend the Sabah Scout Council meeting in Kota Kinabalu. It was a wonderful experience for me as a greenhorn to sit amongst the leaders of the scouting fraternity. Throughout the tenor of my scouting activities in the teachers training college, we embarked on several outdoor activities such as camping on Gaya Island and hitchhiking to Papar, beside the normal scouting activities in the college.

P13:From left Mr Michael Majon,Mr Ang our
lecturer and Bryan Paul lai(author)
Having a tea break

Gaya Island escapade.

*D*uring our Gaya Island camping, the Marine Department of Kota Kinabalu provided us the Marine Boat to cross the bay from Kota Kinabalu to Gaya Island.

Unfortunately Gaya Island had no jetty to berth the boat, so we had to utilize a small canoe to ferry all our belongings. The other scouters had to swim to the shore. We were lucky no one was hurt due to the risk that lay in wait amongst the coral reefs.

We camped on Gaya Island for the night and coincidentally met our art lecturer, Mr Voo, who was also camping there. It was a wonderful evening as we built a big campfire and sang most of the scout songs under the silhouette of the evening dusk.

Early the following morning, we had a ceremonial flag raising ceremony and sang the national anthem before we proceeded to prepare for our round trip of Gaya island sojourn.

We had a short break for breakfast followed by a final discussion with each patrol leader to lay out the distance and time it would take to circle the island within a day. After getting all our gear and other necessary tools ready, we were divided into two groups. Each would begin in the opposite direction and were expected to return before at dusk.

Our journey started off well and everyone was enjoying the walk by the side of the sandy beach with no obstacles whatsoever. It was not until the far end of the island when we could not proceed due to the steep cliff. We had to either walk in the deep sea water or climb the steep hill and walk through thick thorny bushes. After a short discussion, we agreed to walk in the chest-high water along the beach. It was fine until at the further end when the water suddenly became neck-high. Poor Azis Assah who was the shortest had to struggle and swim with all his belongings submerged. He had to cling to us to stay afloat. However, we finally reached the other end of the beach at the expense of my camera which could not be used anymore.

After changing into dry clothes, we continued our journey. It was already late and by the time we reached only two third of the journey, it was already dark. We were so tired, and hungry, we had no other option but hitch a ride from a small Kampong boatman to bring us back to our camping site.

The other patrol also faced the same problem, but they did not continue the journey. Instead, they returned to camp. What a relief to find everyone safe and sound. After a short dinner we sat at the beach silently, watching the stars and listening to the sound of the waves till the wee hours of the morning. The only damper to my happiness was that my only camera that I had bought from Uncle George Chin was completely useless.

The next day we left by the marine boat after cleaning up the debris along the beach, as we were very concerned about our environment.

Hiking to Buang Sayang Beach from Kota Kinabalu to Papar..

*O*ur second epic journey was to attempt to walk to Papar from Kota Kinabalu and to set up a camp at the Papar Buang Sayang Beach.

The senior boy scouts taking a short rest before entering the railway tunnel

We tracked along the railway line as our reference, and started the journey from the Tanjung Aru Train Station Kota Kinabalu. Out of the fifteen participants, only half were able to make the journey on foot while the rest had to take the train ride. The second group led by Ng Thien Sung had to hitch a ride from the approaching train. They were extremely exhausted and had blisters and sores on their feet. Finally, they reached Papar. Feeling more energetic, they continued walking to the beach which took them about an hour to reach there.

Those of us who continued on foot only managed to arrive at the beach at around six in the evening. Imagine how grateful we were for the train ride party who had pitched up the tent and gotten ready food and drinks for us. They had also gathered up enough wood for the night campfire and dug the temporary toilet.

We camped for three days and two nights at the beach. During the night we had our campsite lighted by the flames of the campfire, as the full moon beamed at us throughout the dark starless night. The tide was high and the waves kept on licking the wide sandy beach. Our camping expedition went off smoothly and all of us returned by train to Kota Kinabalu. I managed to meet my old pal Mr. Lee Fah Sing, the manager of HSBC Papar.

The Gaya College scout troop resting after a long walk 1968
Kota Kinabalu Sabah Malaysia

The Scout group waiting to hitch a ride from the train

My secret aficionado.

*O*ur college activities continued unhindered, as all the scheduled teaching practice where trainees would be posted to various schools in Kota Kinabalu were finalized. We were so engrossed with our day-to-day activities that we did not realize the college examination was just around the corner.

Meanwhile, I had fallen in love with a Tawau girl named Lilian Koh. My relationship with Lilian had gone strong with some hiccups along the way. During the first term holiday at the end of 1967, I went to Lilian's house in Kampong Ice Box. Her house was situated by the side of the road. The rear of the house was situated right on the beach.

Lilian stands in front of her house at Kampung Ice Box.

It was my first encounter with the parents. I did not enter the house, but stood outside waiting for her. Her father was sitting outside, repairing some fishing nets. This old fisherman, Mr. Koh Bak Chin and his ten children were in Sabah at the turn of the century. Most of the children were born in Tawau of seven boys and three girls. Throughout his life, he was involved in the fishing industry. He owned several boats and Kilong (fish trap) in the open water in front of Tinagat area, not knowing that one day I would marry his daughter They also had a fish outlet at the Tawau fish market.

It was a very big family where several of his elder children were helping him in the fishing enterprise.. His first house was on the seafront at jalan Chester but it was completely destroyed during the great fire in 1953. They then moved to Kampung Tintingan and lived there since. They moved out from the beach front house in 1968.. Lillian was the youngest in the family.

The mystery ball

I was at Lillian house waiting to take her out, when I noticed a round object made entirely out of glass lying amongst the rubbish and some unusable nets. I was curious and touch it, when out of the blue came an idea in my mind. Wouldn't it be attractive, I thought to myself, if I could turn the glass ball into a bedside lamp. Lilian was by my side so I took the chance to ask her father whether he need the ball. He told me that he found the ball in the sea whilst fishing. He had no need for it, and I could take it away. I took it straight away, and placed it in my car.

When I reached my home in Tinagat, I put it in our fish aquarium. By coincidence, the ball seemed to follow us whenever we moved from house to house till we lived in Taman Bestari Tawau. Somehow, while unpacking, the glass ball would be found nestled among all the packed items.

My initial idea of making it into a bedside lamp suddenly had to be abandoned. It happened when one day, upon clearer inspection, the children saw that there was an insignia in Chinese that meant 'Angel' printed on the slightly protruding tip of the ball. It was a strange mark. My family and I debated whether to get rid of it or keep it. In the end, we decided to keep it and let it remain as it was from the day I took it from the beach. Hopefully the mark signifies good fortune to the family who keeps it. Now, the ball glass is still with the family. I hope one day someone would solve the mystery of the glass ball for us.

The mysterious glass ball and at one of the right 'eyes',
written in Chinese an insignia meaning 'Angel'.

Our final teaching practice

$\mathcal{B}$oth Lilian and I managed to complete our practical teaching and academic performance without any referral.

Both of us were posted to SRK Tanjung Aru. She had to deal with hyperactive international pupils.

Lilian first teaching practice at SRK Tanjung Aru in 1967 Kota Kinabauy
Confronted with pro active pupils

Lillian at her teaching practice at SRK Tanjung Aru. She was having a hard time controlling the international pupils.

Countdown for Service and Trading

$\mathcal{M}$eanwhile, in Tawau, Service and Trading had focused its main business to timber and had moved its operation to Bohor in Indonesia. With the trading business not doing well, Service and Trading, had to cease operation and all good, stock and barrel were sold at a bargain' price. Dad continued his dealing with the Indonesian timber enterprise. There were some minor problems with the Japanese company and the money which should be forthcoming did not materialize. After waiting for more than a year, dad finally realized that the deal had gone sour.

Dad began to think of other business enterprise. After much thought he started a small coconut oil factory at Tinagat.. My brother Raphael left his job at the Chartered Bank to help dad out at his factory. Raphael did the purchasing of coconuts and after it was processed, sold them to shops around town as a fresh coconut oil. Business was quite good. Dad managed to sustain his family with the income of the factory.

However, five years later, dad decided to sell the whole machinery and business to Dato Eransa of Semporna. Raphael got a job in Amalina Plantation, Lahad Datu while dad decided to take a much needed break.. Several years later, Raphael left this job and came back to Tinagat.

The Seaweed Farm

*W*ith not much to do, Dad and Raphael decided to venture into the seaweed farm. After a proper investigation of the location and water suitability, they decided to place the farm close to Timbun Mata. The site was suitable as it was quite near to Sitangkai in the Philippines and the seaweed cuttings could easily be obtained from the sea around that location. Several months later, after the whole preparation of getting a temporary permit to occupy the sea was approved. They bought all the necessary materials and boats.

The weed farming enterprise at Semporna hamlet close to setengkal Philippine 1985 Workers at work for the sheltor.

The hut in the middle of the seaweed farm in Semporna sea.

The farm was progressing well and some weeds were harvested and dried. However, the volume was not big enough to export. As the months passed by, several unexpected problems arose, and they barely had enough financial means to sustain the operation. The greatest problems to the farm were the sea turtles and *Ikan Blias*. These two creatures could destroy the whole farm in just one night.

However, the straw that broke the camel's back was the constant danger of facing heavily armed marauding pirates who would come to take shelter during stormy weathers. Although they would not harm anyone, they would occasionally take off with the entire food ration meant for the workers.

With no financial backing from any other sources, Peter found it difficult to sustain the business and decided to cease operation for good. Dad finally retired and Raphael my brother continued with his unsettling effort in life.

Searching for family clan

My Paternal Grandfather

*S*everal months before I returned to Tawau after finishing my stint in college, I went on a quest to seek as much information as possible on the Lai Clan's background in Kota Kinabalu. Dad had always been secretive about his past and did not provide us any information about his family clan. I had been kept in the dark for all those years, ever since we were in Wallace Bay. I was curious to know and to find out my father's family roots. After meeting my uncle Patrick, uncle Anthony and Aunty Rose Fung, a clearer picture gradually emerged and I finally understood why my father Peter had never spoken about his family clan.

The Lai Clan taken in Papar North Borneo in 1920s

Austin Lai Man @ Lai Yao Leong was brought to Borneo by his mother, Mary Lim at an early age, so young that he was still depending on his mother's milk. My great grandfather Lai Vui Yin died in China in Kwang Thung Province. He was a building contractor and was an expert in explosive which was given the name of Sang Lu Pan. His unexpected death gave rise to various problems that prompted Mary Lim to search for a sanctuary to escape from the family's grapple, mainly due to unsettled family property issues. As a woman, she had no right on any of the inheritance. She had no other alternative but to bring her children to Hong Kong and took refuge at the Catholic Mission.

In Hong Kong at the Catholic mission, they were baptized and became Christians. Eventually, they followed an exodus of migrants to Borneo to work as laborers, encouraged by the British. There were seven of them in the family. The eldest being Lai Ah Yu, followed by Lai Ah Fatt, Lai Ah Phan and Lai Man or Austin Lai Yao Leong. The two girls were Lai Thiam Tai, and Lai Ah Gan.

Lai Thiam Tai's family, spouse Fung Tai in Sandakan
(Simon, son of Lai Thiam Tai became the first
local Catholic Bishop in Sabah)

The Fung Tai Clan in Sandakan spouse of Lai Thiam Tai.

It was a daunting task for Mary Lim to travel to such a long distance in such circumstances. She decided to bring her two sons Lai Pan and Lai Man, and left Lai Fatt with the two younger girls as a surety of their safety. After she had arrived in Borneo safe and sound, the rest of her children - Lai Ah Yu, Lai Ah Fatt and two other girls, Lai Thiam Tai and Lai Ah Gan followed suit. They made a home in a small hamlet at Kampung Mangis, Papar. I could not ascertain which school they studied with, but I presume it was probably Sacred Heart Primary School.

My grandfather Austin Lai Man @ Lai Yao Leong was attached at the only railway department in North Borneo. He was one of the station masters and served in Jesselton, Papar, Beaufort and Keningau in 1918.

Eventually, Lai Fatt stayed put in Papar, whilst Lai Phan went to Sandakan and Lai Man in Jesstelton working as a Station Master at the one and only British Railway. Austin Lai Man married Magdalena Yapp Nyuk Lan, a sino-kadazan lass. They had seven children, five boys and two girls, namely Joseph Lai Kui Choi the eldest, followed by Theresa Lai Kui Yin, Peter Raymond Lai Kui Fook, Paul Lai Kui Siong, Simon Lai Kui Fatt, Anthony Lai Kui Yu and the youngest girl, Theresa Lai Kui Chu (known as the younger Theresa).

Magdalena Yapp Nyuk LAN, died of a complicated childbirth at thirty-six years of age. She was buried at the Linkungan Cemetery in Beaufort. Austin Lai later married a Miss Liow and they had a child, who sadly, died several months later. She too passed away two years later. It was during this time that the four grown children, namely Joseph, Theresa, Peter, and Paul were sent to Sandakan and placed into the boarding house at St Mary Sandakan. The three younger ones, Simon, Anthony and young Theresa were left in Kota Kinabalu. Austin eventually remarried another young lass by the name of Miss Chu, and had three children - Philomenia Lai Kui Ching, Francis Lai Kui Phui and Patrick Lai Kui Sinn.

The four children in Sandakan continued their schooling till the Second World War which started in 1941. That was the moment when my father, Peter Raymond Lai, who worked at the Sandakan Civil Hospital as a dresser, met and fell in love with my mother Gabriela Remedia Lobos, who was from a different ethnic tribe. He married her without the old man's blessing. Perhaps it was due to his contempt for the old man that the family distanced themselves from Peter. Peter left Sandakan to Tongod in the Kinabatangan prefecture, then to Jesselton before leaving for Lahad Datu.

Austin Lai Man's children

*O*n my father's side of the Lai family, the first uncle that I got to meet was my uncle Joseph Lai in 1957, when he was transferred to Tawau working for the Public Works department. He helped dad to design his first house at Jalan Kuhara. I was then staying in the boarding house and took the opportunity to visit him and to meet his children Agnes, William and Jerome. Several years later, he was transferred back to Kota Kinabalu and we lost touch. I was told he had died in Singapore in 1978 and the whole family had migrated to Australia.

The eldest son Joseph Lai

Portrait of Joseph Lai and family taken in Tenom.
Agnes, his eldest daughter, is not in the picture

The second relative from the Lai clan that I met was my uncle Paul Lai in 1965, on my returned from Kuala Lumpur. I spent a few days in Kota Kinabalu and had the opportunity to meet my uncle Paul Lai in Tuaran. He was attached at the Tuaran District Office as a District Officer. He was kind enough to bring me around Tuaran town and showed me around at the cattle farm. I met his children, Clara, Felix, Edward and Maureen

My cousin Felix took me around Kota Kinabalu and to La Salle School to witness the Parliament proceeding run by the students as a training ground for future leaders.

A grandaunt I also had the opportunity to meet was Aunty Rose Fung and husband Peter Chia when he was on duty in Tawau in 1964. However, he left Tawau several years later. It was also during this year that I met another uncle by the name of Patrick Lai, who was working as a cadet planter at Borneo Abace and later left Tawau to work in Kota Kinabau, and subsequently went to Singapore for further studies.

It was a daunting task to search for the real picture of the Lai family, but I knew I could start by getting in touch with those whom I knew.

I started with the relatives whom I got to know about in Kota Kinabalu. With Aunty Rose Fung's help, I was able to find the missing pieces of the puzzle one at a time. I travelled to Papar to try and meet the old man Lai Fatt, my granduncle; my grandfather's eldest brother in his home close to the St Joseph church. Armed with a bottle of wine, I went to his house. Unfortunately, he was not in, so I sat at the staircase and waited for him to return. After waiting fruitlessly for more than an hour, I decided to leave. However, I left the bottle of wine on the stairs without noting the source. Probably he might have thought it was a gift from heaven.

I had no knowledge at that time that my father had an elder sister by the name of Theresa Lai Kui Yin and who was staying close by to the Sacred Heart Church. Her husband Mr. Tung had been called by the Lord when this photo was taken. It would have been refreshing to meet all my first cousins, but the opportunity to inculcate closer ties was very reclusive.

Another brother of my father by the name of Anthony Lai, attached to the Sabah Electricity Board, was also staying in Kota Kinabalu, but again, I failed to meet his family.

The only family that I visited quite often was Mr and Mrs Peter Chia. He was attached at the telecom department in Kota Kinabalu and wife Rose Fung was a house wife. I was acquainted with them while Peter was working in Tawau in 1963. They lived close to the KK airport at Tanjung Aru. During my years in college in 1967 and 1968, I used to visit the family and spend my time with them and their daughter Cabrini.

Mr Peter Chia, wife Rose Fung and daughter Cabrini Chia

Occasionally I could meet my Uncle Patrick Lai the director of social welfare and Aunty Agatha, who worked at the State Public Library. My uncle Anthony, Philomena Lai Kui Ching and Francis Lai Kui Phui had been very elusive and I had no opportunity to meet their family. Much of the family clan history was given to me by Uncle Patrick and Aunty Rose. I began to understand that my father's clan was very much bigger than I had initially thought. Beside the above, my uncle Simon, who worked in Lamag died at an early age of 23 years in 1949.

15.09.2002   Patrick Lai and family

Standing L – R Charles, Danny, Catherine
Seated   L – R Denise, Patrick, Agatha, Se[

Mr Patrick Lai, Agata Voo and family in Kota Kinabalu

My Maternal Grandfather on my mother's side.

*V*asinta Salvador is my great great grandmother who took her children to Sandakan during the Spanish American War. Clara is my grandmother married to Valentino Villalobos in Sandakan

Vasinta Salvador and her children
Clara, Pablo and Clara from the Philippines 1887
that migrated to Sandakan in 1902

I did not know much of the mother's clan either until I met my paternal grandfather, Valentino Villalobos. At that time, we were living in Wallace Bay. He arrived at Wallace Bay unexpectedly in 1952. He had travelled all the way from Sandakan on a steamship and landed in Tawau, not knowing a single soul. He was fortunate that upon his inquiry, he mentioned the name of Peter Raymond Lai. One of the boatmen of the launches heard him mentioning my father's name and immediately put him on one of the boats bound for Wallace Bay.

The boat arrived late in the evening. We had just finished our dinner when he appeared suddenly at our door, feeling exhausted, thirsty and hungry as he had been travelling the whole day with no money. Fortunately, we had some food still available in the food cabinet. My mom quickly prepared some food for her starving father.

My grandfather stayed with us for several months before he decided to return to Sandakan. At that time, I had been recuperating for more than a year after being sick at the boarding house at Holy Trinity School Tawau in 1950. My parents had decided not to send me back to the same school. Finally, they agreed to let me go together with my grandfather to Sandakan and to study at St Mary Primary School. We travelled by ship back to Sandakan, accompanied by my mom. I was restless and decided to fly a piece of paper attached to a string and put it out the ship's porthole. Suddenly the wind blew the cover of the pothole and slump on my finger. The blood came out profusely, grandpa as usual, applied the village remedy by putting some coffee, and bandage my hand with a handkerchief.

My mother's clan in Sandakan
My mother's father Villalobos, her sisters and the
children taken in Sandakan in 1948.

When we arrived in Sandakan, I was brought to the dispensary to get my wounds properly dressed.. Fortunately, my aunty Elsie, my mother's youngest sister was working at the clinic. After the dressing, we went directly to Kampung Gulam to stay at my granduncle Pablo Delgado's house by the seaside. I was surprised that my mother has so many sisters and relatives in Sandakan, the place where I was born during the war in 1943.

My two years in Sandakan gave me the opportunity to meet many of my mother's family, such as the Tan, the Brand, the Bazan, the Simen and the Arguellies and it was uplifting on my part to know that I have so many relatives. In actual fact, I also had a granduncle by the name of Lai Phan, and a grandaunt who married Fung Tai in Sandakan. They were my paternal grandfather's siblings, but we never had the chance to get acquainted and I did not even know of their existence at that time.

My curiously to probe into the lives of the family clan had somewhat enlighten my understanding about my background, and hopefully would be able to build bridges between the family members. Besides that, as a part of a family clan, it is always good to know the people whom we are linked to in one way or another. By getting to know them, we would be able to form a cordial relationship within our family clan, and would even be able to provide solace in time of tribulation faced from time to time.

Final year at Gaya College

*A*fter spending two solid years in college and completed all the teaching practices and academic requirement, we returned to our home town. We were given the options by the department to travel home either by ship or by plane. After a brief discussion with my girlfriend Lilian, we decided to travel by boat to gain some experience travelling on board the ship.

I went to the travel agency of Harrison and Crosfield and met with the officer in charge, Mr. Victor Lim, an old friend from Sandakan. We were given a second class booth at the rear end of the ship. We travelled by SS Kimanis, a steamship that travelled all along the coast, bringing in goods and supplies to several coastal towns in Sabah. I had been travelling many times on board ships and would not be affected by the stormy weather. Unfortunately, poor Lilian had no experience in such conditions and had to bear the brunt of seasickness throughout the journey

I enjoyed every bit of the journey; feeling completely relaxed and was able to savor each experience. I loved to hear the bell of the Chinchu (ship's cook) calling the passengers for lunch or dinner. The table setting was western style. The beautiful presentation of the food always gave me a big appetite. I had to take most of Lillian's share as she hardly swallows her food due to seasickness.

After three days and two nights, the ship arrived Tawau safe and sound. However, Lillian had to take some time to recuperate from her sickness.

I went back to Tinagat and stayed with my parents for a month. I spent most of my time fishing with my brother Ambrose while waiting for my final posting from the ministry of Education.

SMK Semporna – My First Teaching Post

*F*inally, after waiting for about a month, a letter marked "Urusan Kerajaan" (On his majesty's service came in the post. I knew it was a letter of my posting.

With trepidation, I opened it slowly, holding my breath at the final words and was relieved that the department had posted me within the Residency of Tawau. I was asked to report for duty at SMK Abdullah, Semporna. Lillian, my girlfriend, was also posted to a school near to her home, she was posted to SRK St Patrick.

A day before the commencement of the school term, I took a taxi to Semporna. It was a rough journey as the road was not sealed.. I arrived in Semporna when it was almost dark, and could not find anyone in the office or anywhere around the vicinity of the school compound.

I stood there for several minutes, hoping that I could see a soul. There were none. Feeling lost and after waiting fruitlessly for twenty minutes, I decided to walk up to one of the houses situated at the end of the school compound.

I knocked on the door, and suddenly, a young lady with an Asian feature appeared and asked me what I wanted. I told her I came to report for duty at this school. She was surprised and immediately invited me to her living room. Her name was Nana Sakamoto, a Canadian Peace Corps from Canada. She had been teaching in this school for several years.

Nana Sakamoto, the Canadian peace corps

She pointed out that I could temporary stay in an empty government quarter, which was opposite her house. She gave me the key, a candle and a bottle of water. There was no electricity. The school had to generate its own electricity with the generator provided by the department, but it would only be utilized for the student's hostel. Thanking her, I moved into the house, cleaned it the best I could, and set up my bed. The school compound was totally dark. With my given candle, I collected some rainwater from the tank outside and took my bath.

After my bath, I felt hungry. I took out my packet of biscuit and a can of cola I had brought along with me and ravenously devoured my meager meal. Finally, I lay my head down on the clean bed. The journey from Tawau made me so tired that I slept soundly the whole night through.

The next morning was Sunday and I woke up early. After surveying the school compound, I took a ride to town for my breakfast and to top up some necessities and ration. This was actually my second visit to this town.

In 1965, Lee Fah Sing, Martin Ho and I had visited this area by steamship liner to visit the youth movement. We had come to explore the possibilities of forming the Semporna Youth Club. There had been no roads connecting Tawau and Semporna yet. Encik Aspal was the youth leader. We stayed at the Semporna Hotel in Town.

My first visit to Semporna in the year 1965. In the picture is a teacher from SMK Abdullah, Lee Fah Sing, Ispal, Bryan Paul and Mr Martin Ho, at the Pegagau bridge, Semporna.

Back to the school quarters, I was greeted by several teachers of the school who had just returned from their vacation. That evening, my new colleagues brought me for a night out in town. They brought me to the 'floating restaurant' to relax and relish the beautiful Semporna sunset and fresh sea breeze before enjoying our simple dinner. This restaurant was not actually floating in the sea; it was built above the sea.

The following Monday was one of the busiest day of school as teachers and students arrived in droves, rushing to their respective classrooms.

The teachers gathered in the staff room, waiting for their assignment and teaching schedule. I went in and introduced myself to the other teachers. After the brief introduction, I immediately went to see the principal, Mr. Voo, and presented my posting credential.

Several weeks later Mr. And Mrs. Roger Yong, Albert Chung Mui Fah, Mr Raju and several other teachers came. They were my college mates of the same batch and year.

Teachers at SMK Semporna 1969

Teachers at SMK Semporna in 1969, Tawau, Sabah.
Standing from left: Mr Albert Chung, Mr. Lim, Mr. Wong, Mr.
Bryan Paul Lai, Mr. Chang, Mr. Chai, Ustaz Mr. Raju
Sitting from left: Miss Margaret, Miss Nana Sakamoto, Mr
Goh, Mr. Voo, Mrs. Voo, Miss Barbera, and others

I was directed to see the senior assistance, Mr Goh. After a short briefing, he gave me the work assignment for the month. Normally, school ended earlier on the first day of school for the pupils. This enabled the principal and the staff to conduct their first formal meeting of the year.

I was assigned to teach Bridge 2. The majority of the students in my class were around thirteen to seventeen years of age. I had been warned by the other teachers to be watchful of their behavior and conduct. I was trained to teach in the primary school, to children 12 years and younger of age. I did not anticipate having to face teenagers instead. But here I am face to face with them. From my years of experience living in the boarding house at Holy Trinity School in Tawau, I had faced with all kinds of people, including the rough types. To me, this was a small matter and I have full confidence that I could pacify them within several months.

Besides handling Bridge two, I was also given to teach Bridge one. I was assigned to teach 45 periods a week. There was not enough staff to handle the whole student population, so the burdened had to be shared by all. I taught both in the morning and afternoon session.

As a novice of the school, I did not make any fuss about the heavy load given to me. Usually, teachers were assigned to teach for only thirty five periods a week.

My Students

*I*t was a windy, hot day and as I walked toward the classroom on my first day of school.

The moment I entered my class, all the pupils stood up and gave me the normal salutation. The class started with the pupils wishing each other in English, but many of them could not utter a single word of English, so I had no choice but to interpret for them in Bahasa Malaysia.

These were pupils who had been studying for six years and yet their mastery of English was poor.. I had no choice but to formulate the Australian oral teaching method.. It was an uphill task to drum the words in their heads. However, after several months, they had improved, and managed to converse using in English.

As the days passed by, many of my pupils became my good friends. They invited me to visit them in their village in the island of Semporna town.

By the end of the fourth month, Chai, who was also a teacher in the school and I accepted their invitation and finally fixed the date and time for our boat journey.

The houses they built were simple, and many shared a sparsely furnished one-room accommodation. Although several of them who lived in town were quite well off, the majority of them lived below the poverty line.

While travelling at sea, hopping from one island to the next, we met several sea gypsies or *Pelahu* in the Bajau language. Sea Gypsies mostly lived in their little boats. From birth to death, the boat was their only known place to live in.

From island to island in Semporna with students of SMK Semporna 1969

Hopping from island to island in a small boat with students of SMK Abdullah, Semporna

They would bury their dead in one of the small islands, or cast the body into the sea. It was really amazing to watch their daily activities as they churned a living to survive in this modern world.

At the island village with some of our students in Semporna 1969

My college mate Albert Chung and several other teachers were given accommodation at a government quarters at the far end of the school compound.

Mr. Wong, a teacher from the west became my house mate. We both shared the cooking and other chores of our little house. By the end of the fifth month, another teacher was assigned to teach in our school. He was the former principal from Papar.. He was an experienced teacher and provided us much knowhow and techniques of preparing the time-table for teachers. He was kind and was very helpful in assisting us whenever we had some problems. The teacher from Kota Kinabalu became my good friend. In the evening we would travel to the Pegagau Bridge with his vehicle to search for driftwood or just to enjoy the evening air.

SMK Abdullah was located around five kilometers from Semporna town. The road was not sealed and it would take us around fifty minutes for us to walk from our house to town, unless we could hitch a ride on a 'pirate' taxi. It was normal for us to take a second bath each time we came back from Semporna town.

I began to enjoy my life in this simple little town. I recalled years ago when Mr Lee Fah Sing, Mr. Martin Ho and I paid a visit to this remote town in the year 1965 on board one of the SS steam ship that travelled along the coast of Sabah. There was no road or air linking the towns in Sabah yet. Now I am back and observed some improvements to the development of the town. The town had improved and several hotels were built by the side of the Jetty that includes a floating restaurant. The well-known Sipadan Island is situated not far from Semporna town, and is known throughout the world as the best diving spot in this part of the region. My teaching duty in Semporna for one year gave me ample knowledge of the indigenous people living in that area.

Episode 5

The coastal village of Semporna

*M*y first voyage to the town was in the year 1965; we traveled to Semporna by SS Kunak a steamship that travelled around Sabah transporting goods and passengers'. The expedition was to start the establishment of a young youth movement. We were partly successful, but had many challenges to master before the youth in Semporna could formulate independently their proposed youth body.

Semporna, a seaport town lies along the East Coast of Sabah. A variety of ethnic clan closely related to the southern Philippines. In the past, travel by steamer was the sole connection between the various towns in Sabah. I could relax on the pier and see the little boats plying around the bay and the sea village around the locality. High potential for tourism, but was spoiled by several unhelpful incidents at an earlier period. The town was well-known for its abundance sea food, such as abalone, sea cucumber, lobster, cattle fish and many assorted sea creatures that cost as little as a dollar for a cluster of fish or crabs..

That event that happened in 1954 was one of the worst tragedies in the history of North Borneo. The affair took place in the center of the night as the people were sleeping soundly. They were viciously assaulted and several of the inhabitants were murdered by the so called. "Mundu" It was a daunting task for the chief dresser Mr. Steven Jaikul to respond and to attend all the victims. Such incidents occurred from time to time, even up till today, where kidnap became part of the scenario. It takes only thirty minutes with a speedboat to pass the international boundaries of the Philippines and Malaysia, then to Sitangkai which is part of the Philippine territory. In order to minimize the threat, our military had set up a special marine task force on several islands to monitor boats entering the corridors of our territorial waters. Fully armed patrol boats were on standby to stop and examine any approaching intruders. Semporna, Lahad Datu and the surrounding hamlet had been carrying the brunt of these threats that appeared to have taken place from time to time. Government officers in the past were reluctant to serve in the district due to the above threat, but had no option since they were in Her Majesty Service. The word "Mundu" or pirates were the norm word that the people had been accustomed to and would run for their lives whenever the alarm broke out. The town security had been always on high alert for any intrusion by unwelcome intruders, but occasionally the security net was broken and all hell would break loose with people hunkering down for covers as the bullets would fly from every direction.

In malice of these threats, I was not discouraged by this posting as the security had improved enormously since those crazy days.. However, we had to remain vigilant and be aware of the surroundings at all times.

In 1969, the road link between Tawau and Semporna had been established. Construction was underway by a Philippine construction company.. To travel safety, a four wheel vehicle would be highly recommended.

My school or place of work was situated around five kilometers from town and the road was unsealed. We had to walk on foot or catch a pirate taxi. In the first few months in school, some teachers were asked to teach both in the morning and afternoon. As a result, most of us were physically and mentally out.

At weekends or holidays, teachers would retreat to their respective areas of choice. My location was back to Tawau and spent some time at the Tinagat Cottage for a week or so.

On my way back to Semporna, I was able to persuade my father to use his car. This was my first long distance trip and a challenge to me to drive alone for hundred of miles...

I began my journey from town, after ensuring that the car was properly checked at the station. Oil station during those days was mostly owned by Chinese and during Chinese New Year; we had to queue for oil as the oil depot would be closed for several days.

For the first several miles, the road was sealed and the journey was smooth. The moment I reached Balung the road was bad. All the way to Semporna the road was under construction by CDCP from the Philippines. It took me four grueling hours before reaching Semporna safe and sound.

Children of the Sea Gypsies

*M*ore teachers were assigned to the school. The workload that we endured for several months had been decreased. We were relieved and had more time to fully discharge our duties effectively.

During weekends, the teachers would spend their time shopping or to meet friends at the town coffee shop. For hours, sitting lazily, engaging in conversation, chatting endlessly, on every topic under the sun. The narrow street was crowded with pedestrians young and old with unkempt little innocent children loitering around the tamu (open air market), laughing and playing endlessly. The majority of these kids were Pelahu or Sea Gypsy of Semporna.

Watching those kids gave me some inspiration and be thankful for what we are. To put ourselves in their shoes, born in the wrong place and time, life would have been entirely in a different dimension, struggling constantly from birth to death. These kids were so carefree and not besieged by worries as children in this so called modern world subjected to. These children belonged to a native tribe of the sea, spending all their life travelling endlessly between the sea of the Philippines and North Borneo for centuries in their little boats called Lipa Lipa. The majority of them were undocumented and lived most of their earthly existence with nothing but their wits to survive in the open sea.

One would wonder what the future holds for these kids. Most of them were deprived of the basic education opportunity. Would they continue the trend and trails of their ancestors?

With no time frame, they sail endlessly into the vast sea, which they did for thousand of years. The endless tunnel of indecisive future, within the boundaries of the boat, an area of not more than five square meters where marriage, birth, death and all their daily survival took place.. These people could easily be lost in the sea by the onslaught of nature and none could ever recollect their existence.

Such simplistic mind, void of any materialistic desires, except to own the little boat which they have been passed from one generation to another.

The source of their bread and butter basically came from the sea garden bed, making ends meet out of the marine life found abundantly and their basic diet of tapioca cake. Those that dare enough, to venture onto dry land to sell their sea products such as sea shells, salted fish and dry octopus could only stay on land for a while before they get land sick.

Meeting My Brother Daniel

*A*s we sat at the coffee shop looking at the children, I noticed someone who looked familiar walking among the crowd. I watched closely as he walked towards our direction. I waited until I was positively sure before calling out to him. He was equally surprised when he spotted me.

Daniel left the college a year before me. I've lost touch of his whereabouts as there were no easy means of communication at that time.

Daniel my brother at Service and Trading during his vacation in Tawau

Daniel was pleased to meet me, and after a short chat invited us to his house nearby for lunch. We passed his school close to the field and the Semporna Police Station. His house is situated very close to the jetty

After lunch, we sat on the verandah and rekindle some of our past experiences in college. He was lucky to be given a house just by the side of the road and the jetty. The scene was fantastic overlooking the view of the Bum Bum Island, and several islands nearby, but it could be the most dangerous spot if pirates were to land at the jetty.

The house, a government quarter for division three officers had two rooms. Daniel occupied one and the other was Encik Riduan Donald from Tawau The panoramic view from Daniel's's house brought back nostalgic memories of our younger days at Wallace Bay, Sebatik Island..

Nearby, hundreds of flimsy built wooden houses situated close to the Chinese temple and further in another kampong called Kg Simunul..

The local were slightly weary of the kampong due to its unsavory reputation. The wharf was just a stone's throw away from Daniel's house. For just a few dollars, we could hire a small boat and paddle our way into the clear blue sea with our fishing tackle. The water was crystal clear. Fish and other sea creatures could easily be seen swimming among the corals and plants.

My brother Daniel and a colleague of mine Mr. Chai, had been my constant buddy, and the three of us spend endless hours on the hired boat within the vicinity of the sea village and the islands...

At night, the floating restaurant close by was our favorite place to unwind and listen to the music. We watched the sunset silhouette on the horizon, as the waves kept pounding against the stilted restaurant. Semporna was a peaceful little town, apart from the year of 1954 when the town was attacked by pirates several times. Since then, there has been no more untoward incident that I knew..

My canoe

*M*r. Chai was a local Semporna guy. He lived just beside the row of houses beside the sea. Nearby to his house laid a small canoe for sale. I took interest in it and finally managed to get it for a song. Mr Chai promised to keep it safe beneath his house. We used it whenever we had some leisure moment.

That little boat enables us to travel all along the village houses and to the Bum Bum Island for picnics. We used it for fishing and spear hunting during the night. We had so much fun with it that several of our colleagues joined us during our outing to the island for a swim. Margaret, Nana and Babera a colleague of mine had enjoyed themselves, when they decided to participate in our journey. Unfortunately for Margaret, she fell into the sea and got drenched when the boat began to move backward whilst holding the post nearby. Some boys and students of the school laughed their hearts out when they saw the incident. We then paddled to the Bum Bum Island for our weekend picnic.

The sea along the coastal area was shallow, which stretched to many of the nearby islands and at low tide, we could walk across to the small island. From time to time, we could hear some home-made bombs set off by local fisherman. This method of fishing had caused enormous harm to the coral seas and the environment and it was a disaster for the ecology of the fish population. For these fishermen, it was just another method of getting a bigger catch. The harm caused by this bombing method was beyond their comprehension.

Our expedition to the islands.

BPL in Semporna in 1965 to revive the youth movement

At the Semporna fish market.

Mr. Chai my constant companion and I, used to go fishing at night. Brighten by a kerosene lamp, we browsed the sea bed and speared the fish with our three prone spears. The light also attracted schools of cuttlefish that surfaced by the side of the boat, giving us a chance to scoop them up and providing us with a big bounty of food for days.

The challenges.

*B*ack to our normal routine in school, bachelor teachers were confronted with many challenges, due to its lonely and isolated environment. Young attractive students in the upper form could be the source of mental anguish for bachelor's teachers when the body chemistry hit each other.

Occasionally students organize parties in their homes, and teachers were invited as a break to their boredom.. One unhealthy aspect of habits that teachers indulged in was playing cards from dawn to dusk, till the wee hours of the morning. Luckily the habits and addiction died a natural death after several months..

The First School, Scout Movement

*T*he Co - curriculum was part of the education system, due to lack of teachers in the school, the principal was reluctant to burden the teachers on other extra work. So I took the initiative with the permission of the principal to form a small contingent of scouts. The respondents from the students were positive and I was able to form several patrols consisted of hostel boys.. I wrote a letter to the Scout Association in Tawau to register our Scout troop for accreditation.

We began with three patrols that consisted of 21 participants. We managed to function quite well, despite not having sufficient funds for our activities. The pupils were active and responsive towards all the activities carried out.

Unfortunately, the Scout movement was left with no teachers to take over, after I left the school.

Perilous trip to Tawau

*M*y car I drove from Tawau had been made to good use. Teachers used to hitch a ride with me at any time of the day.. During one of the school term, I decided to return to Tawau with the car. Three of my school colleagues, Barbara, Nana and Margaret decided to follow me.

As a novice in cars, I did not examine the car for the long journey. Neither did I send for check-in at the station. A big mistake, which could have avoided.

We started off at noon, hoping to reach Tawau before dusk. The journey went off smoothly as I was driving carefully to avoid the unforgiving gravel road. It was a problem free journey at first, until we reached the Kalumpang Bridge. Suddenly, the engine stops and refused to ignite in spite of my repeated effort.. I was worried and sat there for a while, thinking of the next action. My three passengers sat quietly and looked at me with concerned but not alarmed. I went out, opened the hood and saw that the engine was boiling hot with smoke billowing out. I started to panic and did not know what to do. We were right in the vicinity of the jungle and there were no other vehicles passing by to flag down for help. Trying to reassure myself and my fellow passengers that everything would be alright, I tried to be calm and reassured them that the engine would start.

I waited for half an hour before I dared to open up the lid of the radiator. The pressure wasn't so bad and it opened up with a slight hissing of the hot gas. The radiator was completely dry and water was leaking from one of the rubber hose.

I did not expect any problem, but was duly worried that we might be in a long haul in the jungle. I searched for some water and found some on a small creek by the side of the road. I fill the small container I found and filled the radiator full.

I waited for another ten minutes before I dared to start the ignition. My three passengers were duly worried as they sat silently. Night was approaching fast and we were all feeling apprehensive at the prospect of being left in the middle of the forest with no inhabitants around in case of trouble. There were incidents where people were robbed and women raped along this isolated road in the past.

All the while, there was not a single vehicle passing by, and the three female companions were sitting in the car in fear, growing more frightened with every second as darkness began to fall.... After a short prayer, I took a deep breath, started the ignition and it roared. Indeed a music to our ears as my prayers were answered. We moved on feeling relieved and comforted as we continued to inch our way to Tawau.

We drove on about ten kilometers when the engine suddenly stopped again. However, this time we did not panic as we knew the reason. We calmly waited for the engine to cool off before putting in more water. This continued on until we finally reached my home in Tinagat at midnight!

The car that I drove from Semporna and was nearly left stranded in the unforgiving Stretch of gravel road right in the jungle between Semporna and Tawau (1970)

The three guests were relieved that we had arrived safe and sound. They rested in the Tinagat cottage and went off the next day after a hearty breakfast prepared by mom. The following day I brought the car to the workshop and confirmed that one of the rubber hoses had a small leak that caused the water to seep out. I was so grateful that nothing untoward happened to us due to my lack of care to ensure that the car was in tip-top condition.

Final judgement

*a*fter my car was repaired, I visited my girlfriend Lillian at her father's house at Jalan Masjid. The house was newly and properly built, in comparison to her old house at Kampong Ice Box that was flimsy built at the seaside.

This was the moment to decide the most important event in any young man or woman's life. It was the deciding factor of my life to finalize an event which could change my life for good or vice versa. I was to formally propose marriage to the girl that I felt could be my lasting partner.

We had actually secretly agreed to get married, and had not told anyone. The moment of truth finally came and I had to make the first move by bringing my mother to visit her family. Before that happens, both our families had to be informed of our decision.

I told my parents about my proposal. My father, due to his present circumstance of his timber deal not going according to plan, proposed if the wedding plans were deferred to a suitable date. My mother, however, insisted that we continued as planned. After a long deliberation, my father finally gave in to our requests.

The day for my mother to visit Lillian's family had finally arrived and I brought my mother to her house in the early morning. Lilian's parents and her elder brother and kids were in the hall, waiting for us. We sat for a while and were offered a cup of tea. After a few awkward pauses and glances, Lillian's mother finally spoke. They have agreed to the marriage proposal and the agreed dowry sum was settled. During that moment I was short of cash and had no other alternative but to borrow some money from Lilian herself. Luckily my future wife was generous enough to lend me the money.

We got married on the 27th December 1969, after working for almost one year. The ceremony was conducted at Holy Trinity Church at my old school. I remembered smiling as I recalled this church was where I used to serve Mass for other married couples in the fifties. And here I was getting married, too.

Our marriage ceremony was held at Holy Trinity Church Tawau, Sabah, Malaysia on the 27th Dec 1969. Our God Parents were Datuk Albert Watson and Puan Celestina Tan of Sandakan. Our best man was my brother Daniel Lai. The two bridesmaids were my sister Gloria and my cousin Julie Tan. The flower girls were Koh Siew Kin and Nana Koh, Lilian's nieces.

After the wedding ceremony, we both stayed with my parents at Tinagat cottage in Tawau, Sabah for the time being. A week later I went back to Semporna to continue with my duties and had planned to return to Tawau to request for a transfer through the Tawau Education Department.

I was back to my normal daily routine and keeping abreast with all the activities of the school. More teachers were transferred to the school. The hectic work that I had was reduced to our normal teaching periods that relieved me. However, I knew that I won't be long in this school and could any time be transferred out from Semporna to Tawau when my application for transferred had been processed. Nearly a year serving in Semporna gave me ample opportunity to socialize with the people of different race, beliefs and background. It was an experience which I valued very much. The people of this town lived in a mundane pace of life. Their bread and butter centered on farming, fishing and barter trading with the Philippines.

My one year stint in this town gave me so much joy and experiences. A wonderful time, to enjoy life and took part in all kinds of outdoor activities. The students which I perceive were aggressive had been so wonderful and very friendly to us as teachers. Even when I left Semporna, I was in constant touch with several students who worked in Tawau. One by the name of Ahmad the nephew of Datu Eranza had been one of my best student and pal. I felt sad to leave the school, but had to move on in life and follow the path of my dream

Episode 6

Relieved to be back at my former village in Tawau

*A*fter all the events being finalized at home, I was back in Semporna. My request for transfer had been submitted for further action. I did not expect any problems arising from my request, as it was applied under the preview of mutual transfer with another teacher in Tawau by the name of Helen Mu, who had been longing to be with her husband currently in Semporna.. It normally took several months for the transfer unit of the department to process the transfer of teachers in Sabah...

Back in SMK Abdullah, the normal chores and routine continued throughout the months. Finally, in the month of March 1970, the expected letter came to hand. I was instructed to wind up all my duties and report to SMK Kuhara, Tawau.

The moment to move on had begun, to wind up all my responsibilities. A year in the school had given me a sense of belonging to my students and was sad to leave them. To commemorate the occasion, we held a simple but meaningful farewell dinner amongst friends at the floating restaurant.

After bidding farewell to the principal Mr. Voo, teachers and students, I left the school with sadness in my heart, but happy to back to Tawau. The stretch of road along the route had some improvement but still a long way off before we could peacefully cruise our way at ease. I arrived at Tinagat just in time for lunch and spent a day relaxing at the beach..

The next day, Lilian and I went to her parents' house for a short visit. The family was happy to see us. I sat there just listening to their chattering in the teochew language. I could not understand them until the last word "chiapung"(eat) was mentioned. We took our lunch before we went to the market for some ration. At the grocery store; we saw some former friend and school friends. Equally I was driving back home, I decided to drop by for a quick momentary look at the school that I was assigned to.

SMK Kuhara did not have any building of its own. It existed only by name and was temporary occupying GSS or Government Secondary School Tawau since its inception. SMK Tawau in the past was called GSS or Government Secondary. Its medium of education was in Chinese. In the later part of the year, it reverted to English Medium. This transition was probably performed in the seventies for no ostensible reason given by the department..

SMK Tawau had their classes in the daybreak, leaving the classes empty in the afternoon.. As such, the department decided to get full usage of it in the afternoon, to cater for the inflow of pupils that had increased several fold yearly.. With the explosion of the student population in the district, the Education department decided to utilize any school building within their prerogative in the area..

With several more days of official leave, I took the opportunity of meeting old friends from school and acquaintances of the Youth movement in the sixties. Lastly, on 14th March 1970, I made my first debut to my new place of employment.. I drove my father's car and entered the school compound early in the morning. As a novitiate in a novel environment, I was slightly apprehensive as I viewed the thousands of students and teachers stood round the school compound. I was soothed when I made out some known faces amongst the crowd of staff at the school corridor

Most of the staff was friendly, except few pretentious personals. I, as a proactive and cheerful person had no problem to absorb with the staff.

As the weeks passed by, I started to get to know that SMK Kuhara was known to be an exigent school, a negative perception by the public at large. The majority of the students came from rural regions and the surrounding countryside or were not admitted by the premium school within the locality.. Parents were more or less reluctant to choose SMK Kuhara as their first choice of access.

I was not discouraged by this assumption, as I consider it comparable to my old school in Semporna known to its hyperactive students..

Mr. Raymond Tang, the principal, was in the staff room, imparting direction and other significant events of the day.. I waited for several minutes before he finally returned to his office. I knocked and was told to enter. He was approachable and with an open heart welcomed me. I took a seat and presented my letter of transfer for his further action. He had to acknowledge officially to the education department of my report for duty. This would enable the unit to draw all the necessary records with regards to pay and other relevant topics. After a brief introduction and information on the subject I was trained to teach, he instructed me to see Mr. Chin Yin Chung, the senior assistant to take my final work prerequisite.

After a short briefing with Mr Tang, I left the office and went to the staff room to introduce myself to the rest of the school fraternity. I was surprised to see my old friends Mr. Albert Chung Mui Fah, Roger Yong and Lucy my colleagues in Semporna who had also been transferred to Tawau.

Minutes later Mr. Chin came and requested me to meet him at his office. Looked at me, gave a smile and the normal salutation. He usurped me to sit and asked the subject I could handle to teach the classes of form one and two. After a short briefing went off, and meet my friends in the staffroom then to the canteen for a cup of coffee.

It took me nearly a week to evaluate the students' characters and behavior. I was surprised they were well behaved and showed much respect to the teachers..

*These where the students of SMK Kuhara which we
had to manage in the period of the 70s*

Some of my students at SMK Kuhara celebrating teachers' day 1972

*P3:Teachers mainly from West Malaysia and students
of SMK Kuhara during one of the activities.*

Meanwhile Lillian and I who had been staying in Tinagat decided to rent a room in town.. The distance from our workplace to Tinagat Cottage was around fifteen kilometers away and it was taxing for us to travel daily to our work.

After several weeks, we managed to locate one close by to the Fire Department at Jalan Abaca. Unexpectedly, it belonged to my favorite hawker Ah Sung, who used to sell cuttlefish and water spinach in front of the custom house in the fifties. There were four families occupying the three rooms upstairs. Mr and Mrs Joseph Liew, Mr and Mrs Ahmad Yusuf my brother in law, Lilian and me. Ah Ching the seamstress occupied another room downstairs..

In 1970, my first daughter Marguerite was born. The room that we had occupied was small and not conducive for us. We then decided to move back to Tinagat to accompany mom. Dad was fully committed to his enterprise in Indonesia and had to travel quite often

Peter, who had been travelling to Indonesia so often, began to hold back his travel itinerary due to some unresolved problems. As the issues became more prominent due to factors beyond his control, he decided to keep the matter in view and to wait for the outcome by the Japanese partner to finalize their financial problems..

As the dilemma faced by the timber company remains unresolved, dad finally returned and promptly withdrew from the timber enterprise..

Lillian and I then decided to move out of Tinagat and stayed temporarily at Lillian's brother's house. The house was just a stone throw from Lillian place of work at Jalan St Patrick.

In 1972 she was called up to attend six months of intensive training to upgrade her national language. We were fortunate to be staying at our present house as my daughter who was only three years old had someone to keep an eye on her. In 1972, we applied for a low cost house and got it at the end of 1973.

We moved to our first house in 1973 when Augustine, our second child, was only several months old.

A few months later, I was called to attend the six month course. During my training in Kota Kinabalu, I met an old friend Peter Loison who had been out of touch for many years. My time in Kota Kinabalu enabled me to meet all associates such as, Paul Lim, Alex Chin and his group at Damirka Insurance Co. The General Manager, Mr Alex Chin, a close associate of Datuk Hamid bin Mustapha was the director of the company.

Other friends that I bumped into, was Mr. Thomas Voo, a Karate instructor, short but powerful guy, had been in Tawau before, but transferred back to Kota Kinabalu, Miss Margaret, Miss Yong the sister of Andrew Yong, and another coworker of Damirka Companies in Kota Kinabalu.

With this group of old jolly friends in Kota Kinabalu, we had some wonderful moment to pass the time.

We even took a short holiday at Kinabalu National Park with Peter Loison as our tour leader. Our ultimate purpose was to make a try to conquer Mount Kinabalu to the top of the peak. We had all our gear ready and had prepared physically for the climb. Unforeseen circumstances forced us to abort our proposed adventure. The weather had suddenly changed for the worst and we were advised by the mountain guide to abandon the climb. We were utterly disappointed, but were in high spirit and was able to plan another alternate activity...

It was by chance that our friend, Peter Loison had some acquaintance maintaining the cable car to the power station. Peter decided to approach him to request for his kind permission if we could make use of the cable car to bring us up.

It was a scary ride and very frightening, but was glad that we arrived safe and sound at the Power Station.

We stayed for the night and enjoyed the beautiful view, bracing for the cold night air. We returned the next day with the same cable car and after making some visit to the various interesting areas of Ranau, we drove back to Kota Kinabalu.

Before returning to Tawau, I visited my uncle Paul Lai Kui Siong staying not far from the college. He had an old Austin car which he wanted to sell. He offered me to take it to Tawau with a monthly payment of RM 200.00 per month. I accepted the offer and the car was sent to Tawau

After serving for a year on the job in Kuhara, I was at ease with my work load and schedule. Nonetheless, my old Austin car that was fit for a museum show gave so much trouble that I sold it, and bought a small Morris Minor.

Regretful to say the second hand car had the same problem as my old one. It caused me severe financial constraint as it broke down several times on my way to school. As a result, I was late. The principal noticed my absence in class. Finally, he gave some brotherly advice, and I accepted it with calm and remorse. I had no choice but to disperse it at a bargain price. To replace my vehicle, I decided to buy a Land Rover from an old friend. It ran smoothly for several months until problems began to pop up one after the other and continually had to change the old parts. My finances had been just about the red line status, but fortunately was able to sustain during that month that followed.

Lillian's place of work was quite a distance from our home and she decided to get another car for her own use of a hire purchase scheme.

In the meantime, the student population of SMK Kuhara had increased very much, and more teachers were required to provide additional classes for the sudden influx. As a consequence of this rapid expansion, the Education Department dispatched more teachers to cater for the needs.

One special teacher that came from Kota Kinabalu got my attention. Mr. Stephen Chong, a lively young bachelor, tall and slender with a neatly trim haircut.

I came to understand that he was a former pony rider and was trained as a jockey at the race circuit at Tanjung Aru when he was young before becoming a teacher. We were both in the same page and were able to become best of pal. He did not remain long at Kuhara but was transferred out several years later to Kota Kinabalu and both of us lost touch.

Beside the five work days, which were compulsory, the staff was encouraged to take part in student's activities. Many involved in sports, uniform bodies and societies. Each teacher was assigned in his respective interest. Three years after my service, Mr. Martin Wong, the education supervisor attached to the education department came to the school to observe my teaching conduct in the classroom. Several months later I was confirmed in my post and given a permanent and pensionable scheme that further gave me more confident of my job.

The SMK Kuhara 13th scout troop..

Teachers on duty during sports events
In the picture from right: Mr. Johnny Chong, two other teachers,
Cikgu Hamza and Bryan Paul Lai (author) and Mr Au

Sunday was my day of rest. Simple chores need to be taken care of, that had been overlooked during the week days. Gardening was one of my interests and Papaya was my favorite fruit. It was easy to plant and did not require much attention once firmly rooted. Evening, when the sun had partially set was my favorite time to be in the small plot. Marguerite my daughter and Nana her cousin would be playing around with the tools and were trying to help in the process.

Mr. Pang senior, my immediate neighbor was sitting beside his balcony reading the latest Chinese News Paper. Once in a while he would look at me and smile. In return I did the same, but rarely addressed him due to speech communication. He could speak some Malays which I could understand and my broken Chinese to convey my response.

After a while, he got down from the balcony and watched me with an inquisitive look of what I was doing. We talked for a while and during our conversation, I gave some clue of my interest to purchase a piece of reasonable price land within the vicinity of Tawau..

He contemplated that my intention was serious. He went back to his house and returned with a piece of paper. It was a copy of a land title that his friend wanted to dispose of. I was excited and quickly referred this matter to my wife for her comments. We had barely enough financially to cover up the total cost of the asking price. I reaffirmed my interest and requested to meet the seller as soon as possible. A week later, the above matter was settled and the purchased price agreed upon.

The sales and purchase agreement was prepared by Lawyer Hiew's company and the whole transaction was resolved several months later. I had to sell a small portion of the land to my brother Daniel and my brother in law Mr Koh in order to cover up the total cost of the said land. Several years later, both of them sold their share back to me at double the monetary value.

My wife and I now for the first time in our life owned a piece of land at Sin On Tiku. With the purchase of the said land, our saving was completely drained up inclusive of arrears of our salary adjustment given by the department.

We had no other financial outlay to finance the development of the land. We had no other choice but to obtain it from some financial institution. Fortunately Bank Pertanian had just opened up a branch in Tawau. After meeting up with the branch office, I was able to obtain some term loan to finance the development of the land.

Prior to the final purchase, I brought my cousin David Brand who was currently attached at the forest department Tawau to inspect the land. With his expertise he was able to locate the boundary stones. There was no road or path to enter the area. We had to cut our way through the thick jungle bush cutting all the way with our machete. We had to take special precaution as we entered the jungle due to its wilderness and animals such as cobra, anaconda and wild boar had been seen around that area.

Along the way, I was delighted to come across a small stream that ran through the parcel of land. Water was the main criteria for any successful farm.

There were still some timber standing which could be marketed.. Close by to my area, there were few more pieces of land up for sale. I mentioned to some of my colleagues, but none of them seemed keen to invest.

A month later I bought a chainsaw and intended to use it to clear the land. My brother Raphael accompanied me to the land to try his hand on the new chainsaw. Both of us were under the impression that cutting the trees were an easy matter. We cleared a small area to give us room to work, and then we began to hit the big trees. We started by cutting the small trees. It was an easy job, but when the big trees had to be cut, it stuck to each other and could not dislodge and was hanging precariously.

We had no choice, but to abandon the work before endangering ourselves. I had no option but to seek a professional jungle clearing contractor to do the job. I was at the federal building when I met an old acquaintance Encik Bacho who had his team of workers who could do the clearings. He agreed to take the job at an agreed price and to finalize the project within three months. Three months later the clearing was completed and we did all the other staking and cutting them to pieces by using the chainsaw that I purchased.

There was no road access to the land. I had to get the help of another friend by the name of Mr. Yong attached to the Wing Yew Company to help in the construction of a small pathway.

Then in 1979, my gun application which I had applied ten years ago was finally approved. It was a shotgun and I wanted a .22 rifle, which was more suitable to get rid of the pest in the farm. I went to see an old boarding mate, Clement Jaikul who gave me the necessary help in the above matter.

P5:My boarding mate Clement Jaikul in the boarding house at Holy Trinity School Tawau 1957

I travelled to Kota Kinabalu with my old school friend James Ku Hien Leong and bought the. 22 German Hofner rifle, at the arm Centre in Kota Kinabalu. James Ku Hien Leong contributed part of the cost of the purchase price as he was keen to make full use of it also. With the gun in hand, we went to Balung by the side of Hap Seng Log Pond and did some target practice at the flying fox passing through the region.

The following month, Thomas, James and another brother arranged for an outing trip to the Tingkayu region. We stopped at Balung to get another experience hunter and proceed to Tingkayu for our hunting expedition. While cruising along the jungle road, I was on the deck of the land cruiser armed with my rifle. Just as we were about to turn at the corner, we saw rows of wild boars taking a break on the road. With the rifle on a semi auto standby, I blasted at the wild boars. None was hit, and the boar scrambled back into the forest..

Anthony Chong left SMK Kuhara and was assigned to a school in Kota Kinabalu. Several weeks later, Johnny Chong, a former Headmaster of SK Andrassy School located around twenty kilometers from town was transferred to our school.

A simple and very friendly guy, but conscientious in his work. He had been a headmaster for several years at Andrassy and accumulated an administrator's ability.

The Principal Mr. Raymond Tang appreciated his help and made him as the assistant when Mr Chin was transferred out of the school to Sandakan.

The school continued to enroll more students from every corner of Tawau. There were no classes to accommodate them. The Education Department had to borrow several schools within the Tawau hamlet to accommodate all the extra students. Johnny was put in charge of SK Kem Kabota, Mr Munugram at Holy Trinity School and I was to take charge of our students at SRJK Yuk Chin.

The school at Kem Kabota, where SMK Kuhara borrowed for several years to accommodate the first SPM Students. Present were from the Education Department, Kota Kinabalu and Tawau, an Officer from the Arm Forces, and teachers of SMK Kuhara and SK Kem Kabota

This borrowed school arrangement continued for several years until the year 1977 when SMK Kuhara new building was fully completed and operational at Kilometer four Jalan Kuhara. What a sign of relief, to all the staff and students that had been dispersed to several schools for the last several years.

Our first batch of form five students at SK Kem Kabota Tawau
Mr. Johnny Chong, the teacher in charge at the borrowed school.

Our jungle appraisal

*a*s the months and years passed by, Johnny and I became the best of buddies. Our hobbies were similar, an adventure like me. We both love the outback such as hunting, fishing and camping.

During weekends, we would indulge in our outdoor adventure. Johnny had been living in Tawau for years and had many friends and relatives currently employed in the timber industry such as Brumas, Luasung and Kalabakan. They lived in camps and returned to Tawau town at the end of months to collect their salary. It was during this monthly visit that Johnny's cousin invited him to the camp for a night of hunting. Johnny accepted the invitation and took me along with him.

My gun recently bought had been soundly left in the case. Once in a while I brought to the farm to hunt wild boar or the playful monkeys high up in the trees. It had never been used for wildlife hunting. I was looking forward to the impending hunt and awaiting the day when both of us hunting together in the jungle of Brumas.

As we travelled and arrived at the timber camp, I began to reminisce my childhood days, remembering the fresh open air, the call of the wild, the outback, the jungle, camping by the river side, fishing and sitting by the bonfire, singing songs and sipping a cup of hot coffee reminiscing those wonderful days during my scouting era.

This jungle passion firmly embedded into my mind, resulting from the year in 1947 through the eyes of a four year old travelling upstream the Kinabatangan river all the way through the violent region of Borneo to Lamag in Kinabatangan prefecture.

We arrived at the camp in the evening and rested at one of the huts that accommodated all the workers and their support team.

At around ten in the evening, we left the camp with all our hunting gear and went into the timber track that recently was cleared to make way for the transport of round logs from the Pangkalan (dumping area for logs). It took us another hour of driving before we went into an old abandoned road and began our hunt. We hunt the whole night through on top of the moving vehicles with both spotlight aiming at the fringes of the jungle to spot the animals reflecting eyes.

We returned the next morning with a wild boar on our truck. By the time we reached Tawau, it was nearly noon and completely exhausted.

During that month, we went out several hunting expeditions into several timber tracks located in the Tawau hamlet.

It was paramount to take every precaution on any hunting expedition. Any area earmarked for the expedition had to be studied and must be close by to a big timber camp or close proximity. Entering into an unknown territory hundred of miles away from civilization had to be avoided at all cost. We need to be extra careful as other hunters or wildlife officials might be present looking for hunters who went overboard with their temporary hunting permit. The thousand kilometers of timber road right into the heart of the forest was the favorite hunting ground for the hunters. On any hunting expedition, the vehicle had to be well equipped with spare tires, chainsaw, ropes, heavy sport light and food ration. Occasionally we brought along one or two tents and fishing net to be used should we find a river nearby.

A frightening episode in the jungle

*B*esides the powerful light attached to the vehicle, we had two hands holding spot light to browse at the jungle edge for the tale tale sign of an animal bright eyes. We normally used an open deck vehicle where we could stand and comfortably sat on the roll bar with our guns ready for any eventuality of meeting the wild animals on the jungle fringe.

Hunting by night and entering into the forest on foot would be dangerous and not advisable. Unfortunately, this golden rule slipped out of my mind and regretted of my action.

We were on a hunting trip with the normal companion, inclusive of Buyung from the district office. He was a well-known hunter and had been successful for most of the time. So we decided to invite him on this trip. There were four of us armed with a rifle and a shotgun. After travelling for more than an hour with our normal spotlight, we stopped for a moment at one of the fringes of the jungle. Buying was excited to identify the fresh animal's footprint clearly visible along the road. His excitement gradually grew to an extent where he could trace the smell of the animal nearby.

He went in and followed the animal track that lead to the path in the jungle. He gestured me to follow him, and signify the other two, to wait in the truck. Without hesitation, I followed him, with a view that the journey would be just a short distance away. In the beginning, it was short, but as the track went in deeper, being kept on going into the jungle, with me following behind as fast as I could. We kept on walking for an hour, but no trace of the animal except its track.

We crossed streams and occasionally had to clear the bushes with our machete.

My heart was beating fast and somewhat frighten at the prospect of getting lost in the jungle. I followed him closely, guided by the beam of his torch. I could not return back even if I desired to. He was my only guide to return back safely to where we came from. I was carrying my rifle and it got heavier as the time passed on. Suddenly he stopped and I did the same. At that junction, I froze and waited silently. Out of the silent night came the blast of a gun.

I was shaken up and knew that he had got its mark. I went towards him and caught him cutting the throat of the beast. I was extremely tired and wanted to return to our parked vehicle and joined the other waiting party. To my surprise, he went forward to walk on and signal to me to accompany him. I had no choice but to trod along his footsteps or else I would miss my way out.

His hunter's instinct kept him on the move. He knew that the other animal would be just around the corner of the track of its footprint.

Later on an hour of tracking, Buyung managed to draw the animal hiding in some shrubs. I froze and dare not to move or make a sound. A minute afterward I heard a gun shot and knew instantly that the animal was down.

With two animals in hand the next problem was about to follow. Like an expert on hand, Buyung cut the carcass in two and got rid of unnecessary parts just to lighten the animal. He got some jungle vine, tied the legs together and ordered me to take it on my shoulder. I was reluctant, but had no choice to act as he was also holding the other half. We walked for several kilometers away before we could reach the first shot animal that laid there since we left.

Two blasts of the gun signaled those two guys waiting for the vehicle to enter the path to bring away the other dead creature. For that particular minute, it was a torturous journey as we stepped through the jungle track with a heavy burden on our shoulder.

I had to rest several times along the way to catch my breath. I was drenched with animal blood and had to get rid of the lice and leaches that clung to my body.

It was a dreadful and nauseating venture that I hope would never happen to me again. I kept on saying to myself that this would be my first and last to repeat such terrible endeavor. It was painful for me to envisage the terrible incident. This experience would keep me away from intruding into the jungle on foot during night time as long as I exist.

It got several months before we started out our hunting trips again and it had to be on a safari hunting mission. This was the only safe method of a happy hunting trip.

The wildlife officials of the forestry department had a daunting job of overseeing the thousand kilometers of jungle track of timber roads crisscrossing the forest proper.

The Tawau hamlet had two breeds of hunters. One was to take every opportunity to hunt for wildlife for economic reason. The other group was to take as a game on weekend sojourn. We were a part of the latter group. Our team usually consisted of Johnny Chong, Roger Yong, Albert Chia, Abdul Malik from vocational school, Ah Tai, James Ku, Thomas Ku, Daniel, Raphael, Clement Jaikul, Buyung, the district office driver, Michael Watson from Kunak, Lo Ah Pan, Heron Paul Berry and others that pop up from time to time and on different occasion for a short night trip only.

These were negative implication when an impromptu hunting trip without prior arrangement could result in untoward incident.

Without any earlier arrangement, we took off using Johnny's Land cruiser. We invited Lo Ah Phan to join us. He brought along his shotgun and off we went to the jungle timber track along the Kalabakan road.. This particular trip nearly turned into an ugly incident, that none of had expected. We were happily cruising on the timber truck, when suddenly the driver realized the distinct bright eyes of an animal. He was so thrilled that he accelerated to speed the vehicle. In that instant, Lo Ah Phan, who was standing behind could not hold on and fell on the road with his weapons still holding tightly. He was seated on a puddle of water dazed. Luckily the safety clip of the gun was on. I was also standing behind with Lo and managed to scream at the driver to halt. Right away, we proceeded to help him and found he was not seriously hurt. That incident caused us to turn back early. Incident as this could have been averted if we had applied the proper vehicle.

Penunggu Hutan (Spirit of the jungle)

*R*aphael my brother had also a close call while on a hunting trip. He was with several friends heavily armed and went directly into the Kalabakan prefecture. They were lost for several days and came out the fourth day. They managed to survive by the animal they caught. It was an ordeal when the vehicle they were travelling got a puncture. With no other spare tire to replace, they had to walk for miles to the nearest timber camp for help. It was during this sojourn that they witnessed the spirit of the jungle that lead them to several unknown paths and kept on turning round in the same vicinity. They managed to come out of the spell when they took off their clothes and back to the right path.. Beside the normal hunting friends from Tawau, several friends from Kota Kinabalu also took part in our hunting venture such as Michael Lutam and Kennedy Wong. Both guys were seasonal hunters.

The danger of hunting

*W*e have often heard of people being shot while hunting. In Tawau itself had several cases, especially hunting wild boar. These entire incidents usually were caused by human error, tired eyes and the mind played a nasty trick to the sluggish brain. Supernatural and spirits of the wood were also part of the myth. It was probably due to the spirit of the dead that lay amongst the old abundance timber camp area that was not given a proper burial.. They were buried horridly in unmarked graves to prevent the authorities from making in depth enquiries or questioning the camp management. These were the soul who wandered the jungle in the figure of a white deer or wild boar.

Our hunting expedition lasted for several years. In 1985 with the influx of many teams of hunters the wildlife had depleted. We had to travel further and further into the heart of the forest just to shoot a lone wild boar. We went as far as to Lahad Datu and to Amalania plantation in Lahad Datu District. We were keen to get hold of the herd of buffaloes still roaming about in the district of Lahad Datu, the residual of buffaloes left by Mr Traulson when he left the hamlet of Brantian We could not find any of the buffaloes roaming in the jungle as most of them had been shot by professional hunters from Kota Kinabalu.

Disappointed, we left Lahad Datu and drove back to Tawau. There was no bridge at the Segama River. We had to use the barge pulled by a jack from both sides of the bank. Quite often, the wildlife officers would be waiting at the other end of the river to catch unsuspecting hunters.

In view of the fact that we did not catch any wild animals, we could not be bothered with the wild life personals as they scrutinized our vehicles.

The river threat

*A*nother event that I could vividly recall, was the day when our casual hunting trip to the Balung river with Johnny Chong, Heron Paul Berry and I, was on the verge of being thrown into the river by the impact of a large crocodile on our boat.

We were told that Balung River bank in Indrasahab was teeming with wild boar and was a big nuisance to the Kampong folks. We brought along several rifles as the shot had pinpointed accuracy. We rented a small boat and were going up the river surveying for every animal movement in the bush, taking note of every sign of boar digging up seashells on the river bank Suddenly right in front of us, a lone crocodile emerged. It was a big one and was approaching us menacingly. With two rifles in hand, we had no option but to protect ourselves by shooting right in front of the beast. The crocodile vanished and suddenly came out of the side of our boat with its tail hitting causing uproar at the rear of the boat, rocking it up so bad that we nearly fell off. Fortunately Heron took another shot and the crocodile disappeared for good. It was a close call and decided to call it a day and went back empty handed shaken but in one piece.

Meanwhile, Mr Raymond Tang continued to hold the fort at the new SMK Kuhara School with its brand new building, proudly displayed on a fifteen acre site. With such a huge compound and several thousand students, Mr. Tang saw the writing on the wall, and knew that he would be replaced at any moment.

The formation of PKBM
(Pasokan Kedet Bersatu Malaysia)

I was considering getting the military to assist in the boy scout's marching ability and to improve their performance. The Six Royal Malay regiment, were on their tour duty in Tawau and the station at Kem Kukusan. I made an appointment to see the second in command Major Basri. During our candid, informal chat, he inadvertently raised the issue of PKBM or Pasokan Kedet Bersatu Malaysia. After a lengthy and fruitful discussion, I was very much interested and promised to take the matter up with the principal Mr. Tang.

Mr. Tang fully supported the idea, but needs more clarification from the military before it could be launched in the school. Major Basri paid a courtesy call and briefed the principal the various procedures before the unit could officially be registered. Additional funding from MINDAF was approved and attire for the boys were prepared by the military. The PKBM was launched in the year 1980.

PKBM SMK Kuhara 1980

Mr Raymond Tang the principal, Bryan Paul Lai (The cadet officer) and the proud students of SMK Kuhara. Junaidi, a student was the platoon sergeant

With this organization, I quitted my position as the Scoutmaster and took in charge of the School Military Cadet unit.

Once a week military person would train the students and during holidays the boys were given basic military training at Kem Kukusan. They were given a free uniform and many activities such as camping, drilling, target practice at the shooting range and other military tactics were conducted from time to time fully supported and financed by the military.

As the outcome of this close cooperation between the army and the school, my friendship with Major Basri strengthened. We went out together for fishing trip right up to Semporna and travelled as far as the boundary of the Philippines. The journey had some elements of danger, but we were well prepared with enough weapons on our small craft.

The pursuits of the students were overwhelming. Even the girls were interested and we formed the girl's platoon on an unofficial basis. The boys were ecstatic and many wanted to join, but we could only accommodate thirty students under one platoon. I tried to get the girls platoon officially recognized by the ministry of defense and went as far as MINDAF to meet Major Ning but in vain. It was the policy and standing orders of the army that prevented the formation of the girls platoon.

The ministry of defense did not accredit the group's existence and later, after several months of training unofficially, the group was disbanded. Jude, who was the platoon leader burst into crying. I felt bad for her as she cried, disbelieved at the closure of the girls platoon.

Several months later, I was called by the Military to attend a course in Perak West Malaysia. I was brought to Labuan by the military plane Karibu. From Labuan I took the Herculis direct to the Military Airport at Sungai Besi.

In the camp I met the rest of the gang. Most of them were teachers of the school that had Pasokan Kedet Bersatu Malaysia.

We were totally trained in arms handling, tactic of war, public order and drilling day in and day out. I found it difficult to get up with the drilling and other physical necessities.

Probably it was due to my impending illness which I was not aware of.

A short stint at the Perak Pusat Latihan Askar Wartaniah in 1980 for one month

Officers training course in Perak at Pusat Askar Wartaniah in 1980

Mr Tang, who had governed the school for many years, was transferred to Kota Kinabalu, assigned to other portfolio in the Education Department.

Johnny, the right hand man had to hold the fort pending the arrival of the next principal. Several months later, Mr. Azlan Kinjawan a well qualified officer from Kota Kinabalu was assigned to take over the school as the new principal. Johnny and I briefed him and gave him all the necessary assistance. The new administer Mr. Azlan Kinjawan served for two years before deciding to go on for greener pasture in Kota Kinabalu.

Mr. Johnny Chong had to hold the fort the second time before the arrival of the next principal.

At long last, several months later, Mr. Albert Chia came. Mr. Albert Chia had served both in Labuan and Papar secondary school, a man, who had the expertise and experienced, for being a principal for many years. Johnny Chong was relieved of the responsibilities confided to him. Johnny briefed him on several issues to enable him to have a clearer picture of the school present standing.

Mr. Chia immediately took full authority and several months later began to implement the necessary program to upgrade the school's reputation. It took him several hard years before he could turn the clock around and made SMK Kuhara a much sought institution of higher learning. Result of Public examination greatly improved and after the fourth year, it became a school greatly sought after by parents. The old myth had finally been put to rest and a new era broke the dawn of the day with Mr. Albert Chia fully at the helm of his ship until the day he retired.

Mr. Chia's dedication and consistence efforts, in carrying out his duties and responsibilities were finally rewarded and SMK Kuhara became one of the best sought schools in Tawau.

As a family man, Mr. Chia was very kind, generous and forgiving, but firm in his principle. Another local teacher who was transferred to our school by the name of Peter Chin later left the education service to seek greener pasture in the corporate world.

The school began to expand tremendously with a population of more than two thousand scholars. Accommodation for several hundred students was also available for those staying other outlying regions with complimentary food and accommodation.

Beside academically, the school provides many other activities such as the Military School Cadet, the Boys Scout, Red Cross, St John ambulance, Junior Rotary Club and other clubs that gave the students the opportunity to attain in accordance to their personal interest.

In 1981, I was asked to attend the second military course at Tambun, Ipoh to continue with my training.

A one month military stint at Ipoh Perak Malaysia 1980

A month stint at the military training center at Jalan Tambun, Perak. Bryan Paul Lai (the author) squat from left

After the training I came back to continue leading the army cadet. Due to my deteriorating health, I had no choice but to resign and hand over the portfolio to my good friend Johnny Chong.

After being admitted to the Tawau General Hospital, I was advised by the Specialist doctor to seek further treatment at the Kuala Lumpur General Hospital. I was there for several months before coming back to Tawau.

Episode 7

Back to my kampong at Muhibbahraya Tawau

*T*he first few days after being warded at the general hospital in Kuala Lumpur, was the most exigent time of my life.. My mind was in chaos not knowing what to expect from the medical fraternity. Finally, several months in this hospital, gave me a glimmer of hope on the horizon, as my health improved by the day. The affectionate care of the doctors and nurses expedite my wellbeing. I began to count the days I would be out, and back home with my family.

My perception in life had changed. I am more sympathetic and understand the human frailty, that in the past taken for granted..

It was now 9.00 am and the doctors were on their normal around in the ward. I waited with patience, eagerly waiting for the doctors to arrive and endorsed the discharged certificate. Meanwhile, as I sat silently, my mind began to wonder, travelling in time to the era of 1953 thirty years ago in a small wooden house by the sea at Kampung Gulam Sandakan I could vibrantly remember the solemn words spoken by my paternal grandfather. A. Valentino Lobos.

He spoke with clear, precise words that ingrained solidly in my mind. He looked at me through the eyes, holds my hand and said. "Son, when you are in your middle age, the day will come that you would be inflicted with a disease." I listen with great attention, as he continued to speak. I was so frightened with the prospect that it could happen to me.." But if you survive this ordeal, life would change and you'll l be blessed with all the spiritual and material needs of this earth. That was his last words he spoke to me before I left Sandakan returning back to Wallace Bay in 1954.

My daydream was suddenly interrupted by the presence of the doctors. They came and looked at the notes. Doctor Singaran and Dr Choi were having some discussion with the matron and for the last time, looked at me and said." You can go home". I was ecstatic and thank them very much for all the care they had given me during those months. This was the moment I had been looking forward to. Without wasting any time, I began to pack all my belongings and left the ward in the afternoon. Travelling along with no companion to direct me, I check into a motel and the next day went to book my ticket back to Sabah

I was relief when the plane touched down at the Tawau airport, feeling good to be back at last. My wife and children were there to welcome me. It was a beautiful sense of joy to be home with the family again, after all those months. The wife and children continued with their normal chores and I, left alone taking a long good rest.

A week later I was up and about, trying to synchronies my physical body with my state of mind. I need to return back to work soon.

My house at Kampong Muhibbahraya Tawau, Sabah. With my wife
Lilian, children, Marguerite Youvillea, Augustine, Sharon and Abigail

The next day, I went to my parent's house at Tinagat. They were pleased to see me back and mom prepared my favorite meal for lunch. After a hefty lunch, dad and I sat on the patio, watching the beautiful sunset seen from our house that silhouetted over the horizon. With a bit of luck, the shattered pieces of the past will heal by itself.

I was given two weeks off by the doctor before I resumed my duty.

Finally, as the day came, and my two weeks ended, I reported back for work and was very happy to meet my friends, and the principal Mr. Albert Chia. The school had transformed, there were more teachers and students. The staff room had been enlarged to accommodate hundreds of teachers from West Malaysia and a handful from Sabah. Our State itself could not cater enough teachers, as the student population expanded extensively.

I looked for my desk, and after an extensive search found it nicely placed at the corner. I sat there humbly for a while as I tried to dust off the dirt. The teachers were busy going about their respective duties, and none seemed to be interested to see a frail man sitting on the table alone.. Johnny came, and tried to give me some comfort before inviting me to the canteen for a cup of coffee to boost my moral....

Teachers at SMK Kuhara

Some of the Kuhara teachers sitting in the staff room for an occasion

My teaching periods had been reduced as there were more than enough teachers to cater the needs of the students. I felt, as though I am no longer needed in this school. I went to my former class and was warmly greeted by them. During my absence, a relief teacher had been assigned to take up the subjects. For that moment my mind was in disarray, and was not able to get hold of myself to begin the normal lesson.

The students knew that I was sick but kept silence over it, I took my book, looked at the chapter and managed to address a topic, A teacher was passing by, and before entering into his room told me that the principal wanted to see me. I told the class to do silent reading and would return in a jiffy. Mr Chia was waiting for me at his office. I went in and sat on the sofa beside his table. He smiled at me and asked how I was since my return.

I sat there silently and replied I was getting better as the days went by. I was apprehensive, not knowing what was in his mind for this urgent call He was in a fairly good mood and remarked that my health had improved since my return. The next words that he spoke gave me a surprise, but calmly listen to what he had to say.. With a caring smile, he asked me if I would consider being transferred to another school for a new appointment and promotion.. I kept to my posture, and immediately ask for further clarification. I was then told that the Anglican Church had requested him to find a good candidate to take over the St Patrick Primary School as a headmaster. The previous headmaster, Mr Lin Fen Chong had left the school for a better prospect in the business world.

For the last several months, the Anglican Church had been trying to fill the post through the education department at the St Patrick School but failed to materialize. They then decided to contact Mr. Chia for his expertise.

It took Mr. Chia quite some time to recommend for the reasonable person to take up the job. After making his final deduction amongst several teachers in his mind, he decided to ask for my opinion and note my response Moreover; the post was on a higher scale, which he felt that I should deserve after serving for so many years'. Mr. Chia knew me well, after being with him for several years.

His honest offer gave me some thoughts to consider. I thank him, and requested for a week grace to think about the proposal. An offer, such as this could be the changing tide to my profession

I was quiet when I return home and did not confer with my spouse. I had to make my mind first before I break the news. Several days passed before I spoke to her. When she heard the offer, she was raising some reservation. She was inquiring on the work load that I might have to shoulder and the time required to manage a school effectively. She knew that I had been in a lot of stress and was not in the best of health. I noted her negative remarks, but eventuality after some deep thought, I took the challenge. The next day I informed Mr. Chia of my decision and he was very happy with my positive response. Mr Chia promised to assist me of any problems that might arise. A week later I got a letter from the education department requesting me to report for duty at the St Patrick Primary School. This was the pinnacle moment of my life and hopefully I would succeed..

I settled all my duties and other stuffs at my present school and bid a thank you handshake to my friend and boss Albert Chia for having trust in me by opening up a new avenue for me to prove myself.

With this simple but meaningful gesture, I bid farewell to SMK Kuhara and left the school compound silently after serving for thirteen years of various trial and tribulation that existed from the blink of an eye.

As instructed, I went to the district education office Tawau to report for duty. Johnny Chong my closest colleague was also transferred out and placed at the Education Department Tawau to head the technology department

CASUAL VISIT TO THE SCHOOL.

*I*t was a Monday afternoon when I decided to pay a short visit to the St Patrick Primary School Tawau before taking over the realm completely.

As I walked towards the school compound, a cool shower welcomed me. It was drizzling and I had to hightail it to a shade to escape the rain.

I was dabbing my speck when a male teacher greeted me. Not knowing that I would be the new schoolmaster, he ushered me to the guest room.

Along the way, in front of the school the field was flooded to knee height and several fish of ikan Karuk (drain fish) were found to be popping up to the drainage. I saw a little boy outside playing with water and a fishing rod in his hand. I knew that the boy were playing truant and did not enter the classroom whilst the teacher was conducting her lesson. I did not express any remarks on the little boy's behavior, only later during the weeks I found out that he was mentally handicapped and suffered some mental deficiency from birth. Such a kid needs special school and special attention that St Patrick was not equipped to offer..

As we were walking towards the corridor, I took off my cap and the teacher suddenly realized who I was, and knew that I was the new headmaster posted to the school. He could not recognize me at first as I was wearing a cap. He had been informed but did not expect me to report ahead of time. He took me around and presented me to the staff as we ran into them on the way.. We visited several classroom whilst lesson was going on and ended at the canteen for a cup of fresh coffee, brew by Mrs Lim Hon Ming the clerk's wife who was running the canteen. I thank the teacher Mr. Guok and told him that I would return the next day.

My first month in the school had been vehement. There were several senior teachers currently teaching, was discontented of being sidelined by the mission and the education department. However, this animosity gradually passed away and accepted me as their headmaster. These were conscientious teachers and had been teaching for years with lots of experience

Besides teaching several periods a week, I had to attend headmasters meetings at the education department and settled chores such as meeting parents of the students to listen to their various grouses, a feat which I took it amicably..

My first day at the office of St Patrick Primary School Tawau

My usual morning chore was to visit every classroom, to ensure the teachers were present at their respective classes..

We had our meeting once a week amongst the key personnel to discuss various issues and problems pertaining to teachers, students, and parents. Whatever matters occurred during the week were amicably solved and implement

The school uniform bodies

Beside academic, students were encouraged to take part in uniform bodies such as Boy Scout, Girl Guides and others. SRK St Patrick had a long history of such organization. Regrettably, some of these uniform bodies had not been activated and need revival from time to time. Fortunately a friend of mine Mr. Christopher Chong gave us a hand and managed to revive back the scout movement at St Patrick. With his support and involvement of a few teachers, the scout movement became active again..

Revival of the St Patrick Primary School, Scout Troop assisted by Mr Christopher Chong and his team. Mr Cheong the scoutmaster and Ustaza as the assistance. Sitting: The Headmaster, Mr Bryan Paul Lai and Mr Christopher Chong the district scout commissioner.

The SRK St Patrick scout troop Tawau Sabah Malaysia

St Patrick Primary School Boy scout group Tawau Sabah

Browsing through the staff list, I was pleased to note several of the teachers had been serving on the school for many years.. Teachers such as Madam Ngui, Madam Evelyn Lo, Madam Hiew Ming Ngo, Madam Chu Li Ping, Madam Soon, Madam Chok Lee Moi, Madam Liew Nyuk Chin, Madam Lucy Lo, Puan Safinah Talip. Mr Guok Mee Tong, Mr Stephen Boukom, Mrs Arulnathan, Puan Siti Rahmah, Puan Tasmi Sahawi, Cik Tasmi Palilai, Mr Hussain Bakri, Madam Chin, Mr Singh, Mr Ramlee, Mr Cheong, several Ustaz and Ustaza and many others.

Among these teachers several of them would be under my contemplation to recommend to the education department for promotion as senior assistance of the school. Before that could be implemented, they had to be confirmed in their post. It was a daunting task as many of them were not in that category. The education department posted some senior assistance to the school but left after several years..

My staff at the St Patrick Primary School Tawau taken in the year 1988 in the old school building situated at Jalan St Patrick.

The mission school board

*a*s a mission school, the school board of managers has some role to play and met once in every quarter. The board was governed by the education act with its primary purpose was to provide assistance, except the administrative running of the school, currently under the prerogative of the ministry of education. The school board was presented by members of the Anglican Church Dioceses. The Anglican priest, normally acted as the adviser to the panel

It was customary for the headmaster to be the secretary of the board. During my first meeting, the main agenda that had been the hot topic talked about by the members was the relocation of the present school site to the current St Patrick Secondary School compound situated four kilometers away along Jalan Kuhara.

The chairman was Mr Francis Chong a local boy an acquaintance chaired the meeting.

In his opening remarks, he thanked the education department for sending a headmaster to the school. I was then duly introduced to members of the board. The main agenda put forward during the meeting was the relocation of the school building to mile four at the Secondary School site. Mr. Ken Armstrong the Building Subcommittee Chairman reported that no action had been taken to activate the building fund committee yet. Beside other matters raised, I presented the board a brief report on the school's intake for their perusal It was a short cordial meet and the board was pleased that a proper headmaster had finally been sent to the school.

In addition to the board of management meeting, the Parent Teachers Association meeting had to be called. Another task for the headmaster to perform during the course of his duties The school Parent Teachers Association played a very essential and crucial role in supporting the school activities and the various requirement of the school in terms of additional financial support for school activities and external program. It also played a really significant role to decide matters with regard to parent's teacher's arbitration. The first chairman was Encik Abdul Razak Darimbang, followed by Encik Sabturani then Encik Aminuddin bin Abdul Karim

The cordial meeting was done in a friendly manner and matters raised were the physical characters of the school surrounding and the school field. During the meeting, a member commented on the uncut grass on the field that had been left unattended for several months. I had to apologize for the comments made, but had to inform the members that the education department had not sent any gardener to the school yet. During the discussion a student's parent by the name of Madam Maureen Lee promised to look into the matter and would send her gardener to get the job done. The school organized many activities and parents were invited to participate. Some parents stood out visibly as they took part in the functions. One that caught the attention of the school board was Puan Christina Hadikusomo @ Puan Christina Liew. She had three well witty children currently in school, namely Josephine, Benjamin and Stephanie.

Arch Deacon Yong of the Anglican Church took note and subsequently approached her assistance to help the mission by taking over the chairmanship of the building committee. Arch Deacon Yong was pleased when she wholeheartedly accepted the assignment and took up the Challenge at once

With her appointment accredited by the school board, she immediately instructed me to call the first school building fund committee meeting..

Several members of the school board, the parent teachers association and teachers were co-opted to be in the building sub-committee.

At the first meeting together, she requested that the Anglican contributes the first one hundred thousand for the building fund and she would in return approach the State government for the same amount on par with the church's donation. The committee would seek the balance of another two hundred and fifty thousand in order to start the project as soon as possible.. Rev Fr Yong agreed to Christina's appeal and came out the initial payment to the building sub-committee fund.. Datuk Pairin Kitingan, the then Sabah Chief Minister was invited to the school to witness an impromptu concert and during his inaugural speech gave one hundred thousand dollars to the building fund. With two hundred thousand in hand, the building fund committee immediately began to solicit the other balance of two hundred and fifty thousand dollars from the public, companies and business enterprise in Tawau.

Datuk Pairin Kitingan the Chief Minister of Sabah that contributed the building fund for the St Patrick Primary school in 1990

With a team of parents such as Puan Fatimah Mohd Ali Lee, Encik Aminuddin Bin Karim, Datin Sarah Abu Bakar Tintingan, Francis Chong and teachers formed the core of the building sub-committee

The inaugural meeting was conducted at the headmaster's office with Christina leading as the chair lady. With her enthusiasm and management ability, the committee was able to co-operate fully with her plan.

It took the committee one year to finally collect the required sum from companies and individuals...

The building fund raised was just enough to establish the basic infrastructure for the school building.

Mr Victor Wong from Kota Kinabalu drew the architect design of the school at a nominal fee. Mr. Pang a church member was given the contract to start the construction. It took a year for the building to be fully completed and the primary school at long last moved to a new site. Without the concerted effort by Puan Christina and her Committee, the task of achieving the above sum at a short period would be an uphill task to attain.

The newly built St Patrick Primary School at Jalan Kuhara Tawau

The partially completed building of St Patrick Tawau Sabah

The school canteen which was an integral part of the school was not in the plan due to shortage of fund. After a brief discussion, Encik Ibrahim of Azura agreed to finance the building after it was granted to lease the canteen to his company for a stipulated period of years. The school board accepted the offer. A year later, the education department provides some fund to build the other wing for the computer room and the library.

The Deputy Education Minister paid a visit to the school Reading room.

The school continued to function normally with its new extra facilities and parents came in droves seeking admission for their children to the school. Discipline at St Patrick was manageable. It was quite normal for every school to face some discipline problems. The problem of the matter was the degree and how it was dealt with. St. Patrick had no exception, but it was done in such a way that minimized the problem.

Rules and regulations were an integral part of any institution, society or government, which needed to be followed, but it must have a degree of compassion overture.

Parents were normally advised to be on time, but coming to school late did not warrant punishment such as being locked outside the school gate. Some over zealous headmasters did apply for such drastic solution by keeping the pupils outside the gate or suspend them for a period of time. Such punishment would affect the child's mental anguish and instead of helping them, accelerate their discipline problem. Several years later, after moving to the new site, the school compound began to transform into a beautiful garden. The academic performance greatly enhanced and parents were seeking hard to enroll their children at St Patrick Primary School.

The school beautification award presented by Encik
Mohd Ukong the Education Officer of Tawau.

Several years later, the school environment had completely beautified
and created a conducive environment for the students at large.

Teachers were treated fairly in all aspects of their profession and were given appraisal whenever deem right.

Knowing that they were treated well, they were motivated to contribute their best, to uplift the school academically, and the beautification program of the school. Parents on transfer always had St Patrick the school of their first choice for their child's admission.. Several more teachers were transferred to our school such as Miss Grace Lim, Cikgu Sharifah, Miss Lim and few others. Computer classes were set up and taken care by Miss Lim. The English unit under Mrs. Arul, the mathematics unit under Miss Grace, Bahasa Malaysia under Cikgu Sharifah played a crucial role in uplifting the UPSR examination. With their dedication, the school greatly improved academically. As a result of the good performance, the Parent teachers association with the cooperation of the teachers managed to organize a study tour to Kuching Sarawak. It was a successful trip and all the students and teachers who participated had a great time in Kuching Sarawak.

*Tour to Sarawak Kuching organized by the Teachers, Parents
Association of St Patrick Primary School Tawau*

Lawatan Je Sarawak oleh Pelajar Pelajar St Patrick 1994

The St Patrick students on tour in Kuching, Sarawak

YB Datuk Michael Lim Yun Sang was given the honor to officiate the opening of the mini stadium at the St Patrick Primary School for having contributed to the fund.

Rev Yong Ping Chung the Anglican pastor lowering the time capsule to be left embedded in the ground for 50 years

Students who archived the best UPSR result in Sabah

Academic achievement by the students:
The chairman of the Parents Teachers' association Encik Aminuddin bin Karim, Mrs Arulnatan, Cikgu Sharifah and the headmaster Bryan Paul Lai. The chairman Encik Aminuddin bin Karim donated to each student a sum of fifty dollars for their achievement during the UPSR examination

*The morning session staff at St Patrick Primary
School Tawau Sabah, Malaysia.*

The Anglican Diocese took very serious view on children's education and played a very important role of finding ways and means to put greater emphasis on their participation and problems the school encounter. As such, seminars were conducted to assemble all principals and headmasters to attend such meeting from time to time.

*The Anglican Education Consultation Workshop. Present were
Anglican Bishop Rev. Yong Ping Chung, Datuk Wilfred Bumburing,
Datuk Gabriel Williams, several other Anglican officials, principals
and headmasters' of Anglican schools in 1993 in Kota. Kinabalu*

A year after we had moved in, the school had transformed from an ugly
duckling to a beautiful swan. The school compound had transformed into
a garden of flowers and landscaping. Our program of beautification caught
the attention of Mr. Michael Lutam of the Education department and
with his expertise, he advised us to further raise it to the national level to
represent the State for the artistic and beautification program organized by
the ministry of education. I flew to the national capital Kuala Lumpur to
attend the final verdict of the competition and St Patrick was given third
place throughout the whole of Malaysia. It was indeed an achievement for
Sabah.

The scenic view of SRK St Patrick waterfall and
Jurassic park Tawau view from above.
Partly contributed by Mr. Peter Pang and other parents of the school
(Mr. Peter Pang later became a minister in the State Government)

The Cactus Garden. View of the school from the road below.

Lillian, my wife was transferred out of St Patrick and was asked to teach at SK Bandar. She appealed and her placement was changed to Holy Trinity School.

She continued to keep herself busy by providing extra lessons to her students at home in the afternoon and night to help them in their weak subjects. I was usually in school from the morning till three o'clock in the afternoon. At four I would spend my time in my little garden at Sin On Tiku or to have a game of golf at the Sin On Tiku 18 hole golf club, a subsidiary of the Tawau Golf club. Those two areas were both my comfort zone and sanctuary besides meeting friends for afternoon tea.

After the evening dinner, my children had to attend to their extra lessons for extra hours. Our spare room downstairs was converted into a learning center with Lillian's students taking turns attending lessons. With such atmosphere present within the home, my children began to inculcate the importance of studies and all of them managed to excel in their public examinations and archived their goal in life.

To add to the family income Lillian had to take up tuition giving classes after school and at night time. It was a period of trial and tribulation with four kids to care for.. Due to my illness, I had been away for several months at a time to review at the general hospital in Kuala Lumpur. In the later period of 1985 we bought our first home at Taman Dah Hua two. We had never stayed there, but rather lease it out to teachers and Felda officers and instead living in our humble wooden low cost house at Taman Muhubbahraya. I had to sell the Dah Hua house to enable my daughter Abigail to study in the UK for a year.

In spite of all the ordeal, Lillian managed to prevail all the hardship doing her official jobs, at school, looking after the children and extra time for tuition. I myself took up some tuition to Japanese personnel and others for some English language lesson. It was in the year 1976 with the revision of our salary, we were able to save some money to purchase our first piece of land at Sin On Tiku. It took a lot of effort to begin developing the said land.

Episode 8

The Tawau Sports Club

*T*he timber boom and the expansion of plantation such as BAL, Mostyn, NBT, Wallace Bay, Gurti, Sime Darby and many Europeans companies brought a large influx of foreigners and expatriated to the shore of Tawau. There were no facilities to cater for the social needs or a place they could come together during their leisure time and weekends. It was then natural for human nature to yearn for a place to meet and to socialize themselves in an area where they could congregate during weekends and public holidays. Sixty years ago, the town was just a small hamlet of kampungs(village) with several rows of wooden shops.

Old Tawau town close to the Tawau Wharf at Jalan Chester

The first Tawau Sports Club built of local materials in the fifties.

As the group became affluent, and needed a place to spend their free time to socialize, they built the first clubhouse close to the wharf in 1930.

It was a simple building made of local materials. It was a good place to make available the necessary needs of the officials and top rank government officers.

Then in 1958 as the town grew, a concrete building was constructed with additional facilities. It commands a beautiful and ascetic view of Cowie Harbor and the beautiful island of Sebatik.

The Tawau Sports Club situated by the sea fronts built
In the fifties to replace the old building

By the side of the building, stood a public swimming pool, built by the local council to cater for the general public. It cost only twenty cents per entry, affordable for all. On the top floor of the Sports Club Building, rows of pool side chairs placed side by side meant for members to relax and watched the sunset on the horizon, or listen to the sound of the waves beating below, while they dozed off sitting comfortably on the lazy chairs.

In front of the club stood the Padang (field) and on Sunday's members in their white overall, indulged in a game of cricket. Several would take time to play polo games with ponies at Jalan North Road in front of the old Tawau Airport.

Polo games were played by members of the club at the site of the Tawau Golf Club in the fifties at Kukusan Tawau North Borneo.

Members of the club playing polo at the site of the
Tawau Golf Club on Kukusan North Road

Given that during the time, the permanent structure club had been the main attraction in the town, beside the Chinese Chamber of Commerce. Most of the shop buildings were built of the semi permanent structure in rows. The local traders and those involved in the timber industry and barter trades were the fortunate ones, especially those that came from overseas. In their knowhow and capital, they invested large sums of money on properties and lands. This was the group that was most successful amongst the community.

There was no public community hall for large gatherings or concert. The only community center available at that time was a wooden structure built of timber along the road of Kuhara (Beside Dr J Wolfe clinic once own by Liau Fah of Lahad Datu.

Dancing troops from Hong Kong were the only entertainment available for the towkeys(Tai Pan) of the town that came from time to time. Children were not allowed in as some of the show was meant for adults only. Local film star from West Malaysia such as P. Ramlee and Saloma did pay a visit to Tawau and stayed at the Tawau Hotel owned by Mr. William Thien. In the evening, they would congregate at the sports club and joined the local elite. Several times during the festival, the Bangsawaan group from Apas would entertain the town folks by putting up a stage show accompanied with keronchong music. To join and to dance with them, you need to pay a few cents and select the lovely maiden sitting on the bench.

For the general working officials and government servants, they had very little disposable income to spare. There were very few cars on the road except those Tai Pan who had big American cars. The majority of the general public either used bicycles or motorbike. Some of us used our two feet to go to town. We walked from our school on foot. The solitary bus company owned by Yong Luk was the only bus company that plies the street of Tawau and several taxis individually owned by local people. It was simple and easy going life without the hustle and bustle of a city center. The only activity that kept the town on the move was the musical association run by the Teochu association, football tournament, basketball tournament and the youth at their own premises.

The Tawau Sports Club built in the fifties. An iconic structure during that time

The Tawau Sports Club. View from the field

During those years as children, we used to pass the building and amazed at its big structure and recreational facilities provided by the club. We were absolutely prevented from entering into the club but were occasionally able to sneak in, due to the kindness of the bartender Pacik Utung. The Tawau Sports Club committee had also acquired a piece of land next to the old Tawau Airport for their polo games. The area was first utilized as a polo game on horses, but it passed a natural death after the golf area was fully functional as a golf entity.

To carry out their social duties, the committees organized sports for the local schools and other athletic meet on social function such as Queen's Birthday. The swimming pool, built by the local authority, situated next to the club building and the shore. It had a beautiful bird's-eye view of the sea. A facility, where most of us, the young kids of the fifties would congregate on Saturdays and Sundays. Although we spent a great deal of our time at the Tawau River next to our school vicinity, we were much enticed by the only swimming pool in town which we could feel safe to swim freely. We used to take part in competition whenever it was held at the pool.

*A swimming competition organized by the Tawau Sports Club
and the local council at the only public pool in Tawau town.
The building at the back was the former Sports Club.*

The pool compound was also the melting pot of getting to know new peers within the age group. We pampered ourselves in games till we had no strength. Tired and hungry, we proceed to the side fence of the wharf nearby and hungrily ordered our favorite snack: the famous sotong kangkung. The friendly stall owner Ahsung had been running for years and the best Sotong Kangkung (cuttlefish and water spinach) stall ever known in Tawau. During the Chinese New Year, the whole clubhouse and the front was turned into an open gambling open casino right up the pedestrian walk. Our boys stood there amazed and fascinated at the amount of money passing around. Some of us, although short of coins, took the chance on the Ketam Ketam table and finally had to return empty handed with no money to buy any refreshment. The public, especially the local Chinese would engage in Ketam Ketam (crab-crab) and other gambling activities for several days during the Chinese New Year festival. Beside the normal event, another ethnic group or association had also utilized the club for their function.

I joined the club as a member in 1975, twenty five years after its existence, and took part in many activities such as dart competitions and merry making with old friends. Some prominent members of the club such as Mr. John Reddy a retired planter from the Borneo Abaca Estate, Encik Zaki a police officer, Ahmad Yussuf a politician, Mr Ho a businessman, Mr. Valentine Lingam a police officer and his group of friends aggressively promote the dart games. With their encouragement and enthusiastic, outgoing nature, they enticed many of the club members to participate in the game. Competitions were held on weekends and several of us became good at it and won the trophies. The champions represent Tawau for the yearly clubs meet in Sandakan and elsewhere.

Members of the dart team from left:Mr Lai, Karana, Peter Wong, Mr Arther Jones, Mr Ahmad Yussuf, Chan, Mr Ho, Bryan and others

From left Mr Arther Jones, Mr Peter Wong, Mr Heron Paul Berry, Mr Chan and Mr Zaki The darters in Sandakan for the Interclub meet

As Tawau port began to expand, the location of the club was right in the midst of it. As such, the Tawau Sports club which had served many club goers throughout the years had to give in to the port development. Forlornly the historical aspect of it was finally ended with the demolition of the building itself.

The club's committee had to find another alternative, a site that had been earmarked further away from town adjacent to the telecom department. Nominal sum of compensation was paid, but it was barely enough to build a big building similar to its previous structure and a good location.

During this period of transition, Encik Chau Yan San was the president, followed by Encik Ahmad Yussuf, the Vice President, Victor Raja the secretary and I designated as a committee member.

Mr Victor Raja and Mr Valentine Lingam at the Tawau Recreation Club

When Mr Chau Yan San left, Encik Ahmad Yussuf took over as president, Mr Victor Raja the Vice President and I took the post as the Hon Secretary.

As the memorandum was signed and compensation agreed upon, the club was subsequently handed over to the port. A year later, the club was demolished and cleared to make way for the port extension. The committee had to seek a temporary location to set up a provisional club house to cater for the needs of its members.

It took several years for the clubhouse to be completed and fully functional for the members to enjoy the amenities. Prior to the completion, the committee rented a room on the 1st floor of a shop lot and convert it into a momentary club close to the former Merdeka Hotel.

Finally, the new clubhouse was developed into fully functional premises to accommodate for everyone. Games such as billiard table, dart board, gymnastic room, sauna room, karaoke lounge and even a swimming pool were made available for members.

The club maintained its affordable entrance fee to a minimal to provide for the majority of the young middle class. The Tawau Recreation Club had played a significant role to foster closer relationship amongst younger emerging generation in the Tawau hamlet.

The previous given name of Sports club was changed to Tawau Recreation Club to correlate with the present situation.

The Club with its present hard working committee had given the people of Tawau a refuge for their daily gathering. The club's development started extensively under the able leadership of Mr William Cheng and his committee. My participation in the club's activities began to wind down as I concentrate more on my profession and my work.

My previous duties at SMK Kuhara since we move to the new school were not as hectic as it used to be. SMK Kuhara from its subtle past of borrowed classrooms had blown into a full fledge institution with hundreds of teachers within the work force under the able leadership of Mr. Albert Chia. Johnny and I were able to ease our school workload and responsibility till both of us transferred out to our new appointment. However, we were not exempted from other extra duties such as invigilating public examination conducted by the examination syndicate of the education department.

We travelled as far as Tingkayu, Semporna, Lahad Datu, Kunak Brumas, Luasung and Balung prefecture to conduct the various examinations.

Johnny was normally appointed as the chief invigilator. With his integrity and honest responsibility, the examination syndicate had trusted him to carry out the work without any problem. I was normally appointed as his assistant to help in the work which lasted for a month.

Occasionally, we did come across students with mischievous mind making every effort to cheat during examination, but under the hawk eyes of the invigilators, these students were often reprimanded and amicably dealt with.

During my free time, I used to keep in touch with many of friends from school days and the youth movement. We met quite often to discuss and indulge in every topic under the sun. Several old friends such as Francis Lin, Benjamin Yapp, Stephen, Simon and others met regularly at coffee shops for drinks. Francis Lin, the humorous guy, used to bring me to his farm at Bombalai. It was a farm close to a river, conducive for spending quiet moment of blissful fishing. Francis had a monkey pet tied on the verandah for his personal amusement during break. Probably the action of the monkey made him very witty.

As Tawau was progressing, our team sometimes exploring ways and means to indulge in small business, hoping to emulate those successful businessmen likes Hap Seng, Teck Guan, Sim Mong Piak, Sim Hua Seng, Shim Cheng Pang, Hiew Fook and many local rich towkeys, the old pioneers of the town.

Our impromptu discussion sometimes leads us to fanciful projects such as the Stone Quarry Project, the scrap iron enterprise, but none of these saw the light at the end of the day. Our friend Benjamin and Francis had lots of ideas, but without any financial backing it was near impossible to make it work. Out of the entire project, only one came halfway: the scrap iron project. They managed to collect quite a substantial amount from various corners of the Tawau right to the tunnel of Silimponpon. Fortunately, they were able to export half full ship of scrap iron to West Malaysia. I was one of the members in their enterprise, but was not given any information about the consequences of the shortfall or the financial outlay of the company.

The third enterprise that I was involved was with several close associates to start a money changes enterprise and the Sabah Choi project. Unfortunately, none of these projects ever got off the ground successfully due to several reasons beyond our control.

I continued to keep in touch with my old colleague Mr. Albert Chia and several others.. We were constantly in contact and met regularly at social events and meetings at the education department. Mr. Chia was enlightened spiritually, and was involved in a cell group with Dr James Ku. Often I would participate in their fellowship get-together.. I love to travel and regularly participated with friends travelling at every corner of Sabah. My trip to Sipitang paper industry with Mr. Albert Chia and his group had been the most interesting journey..

Another acquaintance of mine, Mr. Sonny Tan, a teacher from St Patrick Secondary school had been my source of spiritual knowledge. We became good friends when both of us were appointed by the department to attend an English Language Reading Program in Kota Kinabalu. After the training we were both assigned to the Lahadatu prefecture to visit an outstation school at Binuang hamlet. During our chit chat, the issue on Mahikari, Eckankar and Syed Baba became the topic of conversation. I've attended several of his discussion group and got an insight of this optional thoughts and ideas. I took it as a pinch of salt...

Recollection of the past

*M*y recovery from health, since I left the Kuala Lumpur general hospital in the national capital of Malaysia in 1982 had been slow, but steadfast. I tried to make life as normal as possible Beside the project I've just mentioned, I took part in many recreational activities of the Tawau Recreation Club and other golf clubs..

I continued my job in SRK St. Patrick aggressively. The Education department and the Anglican Church from time to time organized seminars and short courses for its entire administrator. The purpose was to keep abreast on the advancement of education currently on going in the country..

KURSUS PENGURUSAN SEKOLAH (KPS) GURU BESAR AMBILAN 9/93
7 JUN 1993 HINGGA 1 JULAI 1993
DI INSTITUT AMINUDDIN BAKI (IAB),
SRI LAYANG, 69000 GENTING HIGHLANDS, PAHANG DARUL MAKMUR

Baris Depan Dari Kiri: Azirul b. Kayong, Sungkit Eri Gilong, Kison bin Saihie, Shakam Thani @ Shani, Puan Moreen Gadur, Ismail Bandi, Dr. Ibrahim Ahmad Bajunid (Pengarah IAB), En. Kamal Shukri Abdullah Sani (Pengurus Kursus), Elizabeth Lok Fae Sing, Hj. A. Latiff Damit, Zainuddin b. Hj. Ahmad, Othman Laud, Paulus Duasa.
Baris Belakang Dari Kiri: Hj. Saidin Hj. Abd. Rashid, Tahir Bandi, Samsir Kasibun, Ahmad Idris, Baharun b. Adon, Peter Mang, Irianto Tarman Bryan Paul Lai, Karim Adam, Jabelin b. Sahjinan, Musa Tampil, Wahid Karim, Wong Kui Onn, Liew Chee On, Lee Chi Ken, Kimpoh Asdi/Martin.

Administrative course for headmasters at Aminuddin Institute Genting Highland Pahang

We embarked on many study tours to many of the states in Malaysia visiting schools and places of interest. My last assignment as a headmaster was being seconded to a school called the King George Primary School situated in Seramban, West Malaysia for a month stint. About twenty headmasters were involved in the scheme. They were sent to a number of schools in West Malaysia and to observe the school management system in order for us to emulate their administrative skills if applicable.

At SK King George Seremban

At SRK King George Seremban West Malaysia

The headmasters involved upon their return had to make a comprehensive report on the outcome of the project and to present it to the department for evaluation. Those were the feat I was still able to participate in spite of my unfortunate bout of my health in whilst teaching in SMK Kuhara. Let me rekindle part of the story that engulfed my life for a moment.

It was in 1982 when I decided to seek medical help at the local general hospital after I noticed that I lost my normal weight at an alarming rate. Mr. Thomas the hospital surgeon admitted me for several days to give me a thorough medical examination. Finally, after all the necessary blood testing, he took a closer look my inner throat. He noticed that my larynx had some sort of growth and advised me to get it examined at the ENT clinic at the General Hospital in Kuala Lumpur. After obtaining all the approval and paper work from the education department, as required, I flew to KL and reported at the General Hospital ENT clinic.

I was somewhat feeling nervousness and stress as I reported at the counter and handing the letter from the Tawau general hospital to the ENT clinic. I was immediately awarded at the first class ward with four other patients.

This was the first time that I had been admitted to very large medical facilities in the Malaysian capital. During my first night, I was feeling apprehension and found it difficult to get a good night's sleep. Would this my final days in my life, in case the medical outcome turned out to be worse than expected. Anyway, I took it at ease and leaving the matter to the creator for his next move.

The next day the nurse took me to the ENT clinic for the appointment. I met Dr Sangaran and Dr Choi. Both were ENT specialist at the general hospital. Both were very pleasant, helpful and kind.. At the far end of the building stood the cancer ward, a ward where many of the patients were waiting for their days. Akin to the final door of entry, an entry of no return was the norm. After several days of intense testing, they decided to put me into the operation theatre and to nip off a piece of the growth for biopsy analysis. Meanwhile, many of the patients in the ward became acquainted and the ward brightened to some extent due to the lively conversation among the patients. Each one had their own health condition. Some mild and some beyond any help whatsoever. As the days drift away, I prayed hard for deliverance. During my intense prayer, the sound from below the building on the ground floor echo loudly in my mind. It was the sound of the creaking of the stretcher wheels on the ground floor, a sign that someone had passed away and brought to the mortuary. I knew this was part and parcel of life where each one of us had to go through and as a reminder to all of us as mortal, that our life on earth is only a passing through moment like the shadow.

Routinely, the nurses were busy going around and checking every patient. I was in a jolly mood to meet them again for their kind and friendly overture and joke that brightened us for the day.

A week later the doctor came in with the result of the biopsy. He looked at me with ease. I was waiting with fearful expectation on the bombshell result. Will this be the end or just the beginning of my life? In a silent mood, I looked up at him and with a smile he spoke with a calm voice telling me that the disorder on my throat could be cured with drugs. I was very much relieved and thanked God and the Blessed Virgin Mary for answering my plea and prayer. I was then put on the special drugs for three whole months before I was allowed to return back to Sabah and to continue with my duties. A year later in 1982 I went back to Kuala Lumpur for a review. I had three more operation to enlarge the opening of my throat.

It was a marathon operation. It began early in the morning and returned late in the evening. When I woke up, tubes were inserted in my throat through a tiny hole and other parts of my body. I could neither eat nor drink through the normal passage way for a duration of forty five days. A small tube was inserted right into my nose as a conduit for my daily requirement of nutrition for my daily intake. With all the tubes crisscrossing my whole body, I felt this was the most horrible time in my life. An experience that charred my mind and look life in a different prospective of my being.

However the constant support and prayers by all friends encouraged me both physically and spiritually, especially thinking of my family and children back home in Sabah.

Finally, as the fifth weeks passed by and the day of reckoning approaching for the removal of all the tubes, I was relieved and thanked the Almighty for answering my prayer and delivered me back into this world. The kind and gentle nurse removed the tubes one at a time and finally all the tubes were gone.. I could watch her face as bright as the angel imposing into reflection into my eyes. A moment later I was given a sip of warm water through the proper channel and several hours later given to taste some fruits and dinner at night. It was a fantastic feeling, an experience of knowing the importance of our taste bud that we usually take it for granted.

This terrible ordeal that I had gone through and facing a period of ordeal and feeling hopelessness brought a new life to my faith and be more caring to my fellowmen. Furthermore the constant thought of my wife and children at home strengthens my will to survive.

Whilst in the sickbay, I participated socially amongst all the patients and kept myself busy in conversation with other patients in the same ward. Some had minor problems and several had incurable ailment such as a malignant ceroplastic disease of the tummy and other sickness. A gentleman by the name or Mr. Liew Yun Loi, a lecturer at a college in PJ became my close friend. I met Mr. Ma, who was suffering from cancer of the stomach, several months later he passed away. I met an officer attached at the Kepong forestry department and several times both of us would escape from the hospital for a day off and returned in the evening.

Upon my coming back to Sabah, I carried on with my duties at SMK Kuhara. At the end of 1982 I went back to KL for review, I was told that my health had improved tremendously, but had to take extra care to monitor for any changes to my vocal cord. I was advised not to take excessive physical activities and to continue taking the prescription recommended by the doctor. I met most of my hospital former friends and we had a night barbeque gathering at Mr. Liew Yun Loi's resident at Petaling Jaya Kuala Lumpur. That was the last time I met Mr Ma, who succumbed to his illness and passed away.

I returned back to Sabah feeling relieved, hope and looking forward to the future. However, this was all in the past and I was looking forward to continue discharging my work as a headmaster until my retirement scheduled in the year 1998.

Episode 9

Vision of a meaningful existence

*Y*oung adults in those days had the aptitude to focus nothing but sports, culminating friendship among their peers and the opposite sex.

Their quest was to accomplish their needs, rather than to look beyond the youthful period, spending endless hours of physical activities taking life as it comes. In contrast to the newcomers from foreign lands, opportunity was in abundance and their capitalist know how brought them to prosperity, without us realizing all opportunities had circumvented us.

Thus, as we approach, advancing age, we realized the lost prospect that could not be retrieved. We fought all the way up to make a reasonable living in our own beloved land.. Some were successful and others had no means, but to wait for the end of the month for the meager pensioner income. Our activities began to falter and the former glory remained as a bygone memory. Our youthful energy that we once took for granted was beyond redemption. The prosperous years of our life gradually ebbing step by step, and was forced to accept the ability and strength that we had. As the saying goes, the spirit is high, but the body is weak.

Environmentally concerned.

*T*he plot of land was all I had, to conciliate my daily physical need. Beyond that, it was lonely, with no social avenue. The mission to seek other scene became more apparent, as I moved on gracefully following the tide of time.

The proposed wild bird sanctuary at Tanjung Forest Reserve Tawau

None the less, it was by chance that next to my area was the second class Tanjung forest reserve, the last bastion for the other living creatures of the wild around that region. Birds of different varieties, such as Hornbill, parrots, pigeons, wild hen, sparrows and animals of all sorts, made the undisturbed secondary jungle as their home.

As I was leisurely walking along the fringes of the jungle area, I felt a sense of peace and tranquility, inspired by the dancing and singing of the birds in the tall trees.

Several years ago, part of the area had been alienated to the Tawau Hot Spring Golf Club and part of it to the Tawau Local Council for public recreational purposes. As a result, the areas that the birds and animals used to roam had reduced significantly and the animal's playing field were drastically restricted.

This area had been my refuge and playground, long before any development took place. Varieties of animals which had populated the area had now remained a handful.

With some tall trees still stood tall for the time being, the bird's had some chance of survival, for their daily needs but gradually diminishing through the passage of time.

I visited the area often and occasionally had some friends tagging along with me, such as Francis Lin, Sani Saliun, Thomas Voo, Johnny Chong, Albert Chia and Aminuddin Abdul Karim had all enjoyed the fruits during the season. The visitors were constantly astonished at the sorts of birds found along the periphery of the forest flying above the tallest trees.

During our normal informal conversation, Encik Aminuddin bin Abdul Karim impromptu sound the need to highlight his concerned and to get the authorities attention to preserve the area as a bird refuge. The group welcomed the proposal with an undefended spirit, thoughts for consideration. A task force made up of the following gentlemen was formed; James Ku, Tadius Sibir, Johnny Chong, Francis Lim and a just retired Wild Life officer. Aminuddin and I took the lead. We got an appointment to further the crusade with the Wild Life department of Tawau. The department was conducive to our petition and agreed to do intensive research on the subject. Coincidentally, we met YB Taufig Abu Bakar Tintingan at the Annual General Meeting of the Tawau Golf Club and were pliable to our proposal. He fully supported the cause.

Several months later, we were informed by the wildlife department that a team of rangers had been sent to the area for a week, to evaluate and to make a feasibility study of the varieties of wildlife that existed in the vicinity. Aminuddin and I kept to monitor the proposal from time to time but unfortunately, Aminuddin who had been the staunchest supporter succumb to his illness and untimely passed away. His death was a blow to us, but should the area be gazetted as a bird refuge, I will propose to the local authority to name the area as "Aminuddin Bird Sanctuary". We did not find any official report from the department, but presumed that the matter had been seriously taken into contemplation. Hopefully the planned bird safe haven as proposed by the committee is supported by the Forestry Department.

Trying my hand on a new pursuit.

J was on my way home after attending a short meeting at the education department. Along the North road passing the airport, a group of players at the Tawau Golf Club was having their morning game. They were enjoying themselves as they continued to play happily. I was curious and wanted to know what the game was all about.

I watched their game closely for a while and thought probably this game might be the venue I was seeking for. Then I resolved to find out more regarding the game, and immediately went to the golf club house to inquire more. It was an old wooden clubhouse built in the sixties. I met Pro Chong, who welcomed me and gave a brief insight of what golf was all about. At the final stage of our conversation and impromptu briefing, I was told that a new clubhouse would be built up soon and the entrance fee would be increased several folds. He advised me to join the club whilst the entrance fee remains at the current rate. Heeding his advice, I requested for a form, filled it up and submitted to the office with the current entrance fee. Several months afterwards I got a confirming letter of my membership.

Pro Chong had an old golf set on the shelf. It was going for a bargain price and I could get it cheap. It was still in very good condition. I bought it without reluctance and took tender care of it.

Pro Chong briefed me some basic rule of the game. Several weeks later he began to coach me the basic tenet of applying the different type of shaft.

Six months later, after spending some time at the driving range, I felt I was prepared to give it a try at the fairway.

Finally Pro Chong took me out to the proper fairway to evaluate my proficiency. He was convinced that I was capable to go without endangering other players and listed my name for my handicap test.

The captain of the club Dr. Thomas took me out for a game. After a round of golf, he was satisfied that I could now play at the fairway without being accompanied by the club's pro.

With that accreditation and as a 24 novice handicapper, I spent every opportune time at the fairway.

My Golf excapee at the Sin On 18 holes golf course

My morning exercise at the Sin On 18 holes Golf
Course at the Sin On Prefecture Tawau Sabah

Many of the players of the club often indulged in varieties of games. As a beginner and a novice, I felt very uncomfortable to partake in their regatta. I would choose to play entirely by myself at my own rate and time with only the birds, the workers trimming the hedges, the blossoms, and the blue sky as my companion and audience. This is the wonder of golf; you could play alone and examine your skill.

As I began to master the games, friends such as Mr. Thomas Ku an old school mate, Mr. James Ku, Mr. Albert Chia, Mr. Johnny Chong, Puan Christina Liew, Mr. Kurnadi Hadisusomo, Puan Mary Yapp, Encik Sani Saliun, Mr Peter Wong, Encik Nista Kabul, Encik Mohd Ukong, and several others became my partner in golf throughout the years. Amongst these friends it was fun all over and we could claim on a casual and friendly competition. As for others, I was not easy to play with them due to their mathematical weakness.

During my time as a golfer in the education department I've played with most of the guests from the Ministry of Education as at that time, I was the only golfer in the education fraternity.

Golf Courses in Tawau

Tawau has many golf courses, courses for professional and for novices. The oldest Golf Club called Tawau Golf Club was acquired by the Tawau Sports Club committee in the fifties. In the beginning, it was a field for polo game. Only during the years, the polo game lost its' importance and the area was completely transformed into a nine hole golf course. Several years after I've joined, the new club was completed under the able chairmanship of Datuk James Pang. The Club House became an iconic building that stood firm and was able to serve the people of Tawau for their recreational purposes. A decade later, another golf course called Sin On Tiku golf course was built at the Sin On Tiku hamlet. It's an 18 hole course which commanded a beautiful scene and environmental friendly amongst the green jungle of the Tanjung Forest Reserve. Due to its undulating nature, there was some reservation on the construction period. Datuk James Pang took it as a challenge, and admirably completed the course employing only the club's endeavor

Besides the above club, several golf clubs were available in the Tawau residency to serve the different level of society.

The par three golf course at Sin On under the supervision of Mr. Matthew, the Kabota golf club established by Mr. Chu. A club opens to the public with a nominal payment caters for beginner players and impending interested golfers.

The fairway was narrow and ponds strategically placed along the fairway. While playing, Golfers had to be extra careful to avoid flying golf balls.

Johnny, my colleague finally joined the Kabota Golf Club as a novice player. Albert, Johnny and I made a good standing group to be able to play on any golf courses. The renowned international golf club was the San Sui golf course. It was an interesting class, and highly recommended for any professional golfers to have a fling.

Eighty kilometers away at Tai Ko plantation in the hamlet of Semporna stood another golf course called the Sigalong Golf Club. The fairway was spacey and with an undulating terrain. There were no buggies and we had to walk, to play the 18 whole course. Albert Chia, Mary Yapp and Johnny Chong and I used to play in the course from time to time.

The Director General of the ministry of education Tan Sri Wira had the opportunity to play a friendly game, organized by the Sigalong management.

The Director General of the Ministry of Education, Tan Sri Wira paid a short visit to Tawau and was invited to play at Sigalong Golf Club accompanied by officers from the education department...

Another challenging course was the Tam Moi Golf Club in the hamlet of Lahad Datu. Albert, Johnny and I had played several times during our course of duty. Beside the three of us in the education group that played golf, Encik Mohd Ukong the new Tawau education officer was also a golf enthusiast and often took part in competition at the Tawau Golf Club.

The Sabah Education department had its sports carnival yearly to cater for the sporting needs of the education fraternity throughout the State. Golf was then added as one of the event during the carnival. The last education tournament that we participated was at Kundasang Golf Club situated at the foot of the mighty mountain of Kinabalu. We travelled from Tawau to Kundasang by road and stayed at Perkasa hotel for the night, a holiday destination to enjoy the panoramic view and fresh mountain air.

The beautiful scenic view of Mount Kinabalu at Kundasang Hamlet

Official duties as invigilator for Public Examination.

*a*t the end of term, public examination was conducted at schools designated as examination center. These examinations were conducted throughout the whole country concurrently. It required almost a week for the UPSR and SRP and a month for the SPM and STPM. Teachers from different districts were appointed at different centers in order to enhance its security and integrity. Our investigating duties took us a far as Semporna, Kunak, Sahabat at Tingkayu, Brumas and BAL estate. Of all the centers mentioned, Sahabat was our favorite location. It rendered us the opportunity, to explore the vast jungle of Sahabat at the Felda Scheme for a short hunting trip. Another center that we enjoyed most was Semporna. The sea food was wonderful and the floating restaurant owned by Datuk Mohd Gan protrudes right out into the ocean. A place to unwind, listen to sappy music and view the panoramic vista of the island and the sunset. Our golf buddy Albert on occasion joined us for a day or two of the golf game at Sigalong and later in the night had a dinner at the seafood restaurant. During our normal chit chat, Albert reminded us of our quest to travel throughout Sabah main town to play at every golf course. This idea had been kept in view for months and as the school term was just round the corner, the quest has lately become more prominent. After a short deliberation, we finally agreed to begin our journey from Tawau. All expenses would be partaken by the three of us. Two weeks later after the final examination, we met in Tawau to discuss the final trip of the journey. We left Tawau early in the morning to Lahad Datu and arrived with enough time to play at the Tam Moi golf club. The club at Tam Moi was recently built and the fairway and greens were kept in top shape. The following morning we left for Sandakan and took us five hours of travelling.

At the Sandakan golf club, we met Mr Paul Chin a long time friend in Tawau. There were not many golfers, and then we had an interrupted game for the whole morning. By the close of the day, as normal, Johnny took in to foot the bill at lunch and Albert the caddies.

The next day, we left in the morning and arrived at the Ranau hamlet around two in the afternoon. We played at the Ranau Golf Club before checking at Kundasang Motel.

That night we had our dinner at Perkasa Hotel. The view of Mount Kinabalu from our strategic location was fantastic. The next day, we woke very early in the morning and directly went to the Kundasang Golf Club. It was cold and we finally managed to get three caddies for our game. The first round of 18 holes was enjoyable and we lost several balls, but at our second cycle of another eighteen holes we were all extremely tired.

We attempted to follow strictly to the rules of golf. Right away and again Albert was not in conformity with our view and declined to support the stated principles. What the heck, we allowed the argument to ease and continued enjoying the game. Albert proceeded to play vigorously throughout, till the last few games.

Golf at the Kundasang Golf Club
Kota Kinabalu

Albert Chia and I (author) at the Kundasang Golf Club
Ranau, Sabah. Johnny was not in the picture.

We had a night of uninterrupted sleep, and continued our journey to Kota Kinabalu the next day. The next morning we were at the Kota Kinabalu Golf Club making all the arrangement. At the club were many golfers about to tee off and we bore no other choice but to wait for our queue After the game, we adjourned at the canteen and found that our game was the worst ever played. We could not savor the game as we had to move fast from one hole to the other. Other golfers were constantly on our neck, and their body language signified us to move on fast.

On our return trip to Tawau, we decided to have the last game at the most notorious golf club in Sabah. The club at SLDB at the prefecture of Lahad Datu called Sandau Golf Club.

It was known as the cowboy course with its undulating fairway, difficult terrain and rough greens. The three of us played so badly and add-on to our tiredness that temper flared up between Albert and Johnny, but I, as the arbitrator amicably solved the argument.

Both my novice friends had tried their best to thrash me, but their effort failed to happen. Eight days of round trip together fortify our companionship. We loved the games and our bond of solidarity reinforces.

Obstruction of vision

*O*n my return to Tawau, I noticed that my vision had deteriorated. I went to get it examined by the eye specialist at the Tawau General hospital.

I was told that I had a cataract and was recommended by the eye doctor to get it done in Kota Kinabalu Queen Elizabeth Hospital. The operation was done, but I could not see anything, although the doctor insisted that it might take some time for my vision to return. They kept me several weeks in the hospital trying to revive my eyesight but all in vain.

Several months later, I had it examined again by the same physician, and was told that I required a cornea transplant. I was sent to the General Hospital in KL for the operation, but it was not successful. The second time at UKM hospital was also experiencing the same outcome. In conclusion, my right eye had become blind.

Family outing with friends

Many of us during our working days could scarcely find time to be with our families and friends. Our priority had been our profession and family and friends became insignificant. But as we grow older, we realized that our close kilns and friends need to have the same moment as our job and need to be cultivated to promote a holistic life. With this in mind, we had some outing to various interesting places within our hamlet.

Our first outing with Johnny and his family was to study the sea weed project in Semporna. Our journey took an hour ride by boat. The whole trip was organized by Teddy Usbah a local who was the man in charge of the farm and the man who had nearly changed the situation of our lives.

*Our Semporna trip to visit the Ko-Nelayan sea weed
farm. Teddy Usbah and I at the front*

*a*s we travel on the boat, I was sitting in front with Teddy Usbah. We had no life jacket on. Johnny's family was sitting behind with the same scenario. After fifteen minutes on the sea, Teddy had the urge to smoke and was trying to light it with his lighter. I was observing him as he tried several times but failed. Suddenly I saw the petrol from the tank moving slowly towards him without realizing the imminent danger. My prompt intervention saved the day and we were all safety back to Semporna after the journey. Johnny and his family were not cognizant of the incident until I told him on our return.. Our second family trip was to Brumas Resort. It was kindly arranged by Mr Kelvin who was the officer in charge. Subsequently, several trips were organized to several locations with teachers and families participating.

*Picnic at the Sigalong waterfall attended by
teachers and families of SRK. St Patrick*

BPL and Mr Guok Mee Tong
my competent Senior Assistance
at Tai Ko P_)lantation waterfall resort

Family picnic at the Tai Ko Plantation resort

Picnic organized by Mr Gabriel of Tai Ko Plantation.

Johnny Chong joked with the ladies at Brumas Resort Tawau

Albert was busy by the side of the pool happily chit chatting at Brumas Resort.

Mrs Kelvin,Mrs Lai,Mrs Ku and Mrs Chia
At Brumas Resort
Tawau Sabah

The four ladies: Mrs. Kelvin. Mrs. Lai. Mrs. Chia and
Mrs. Ku at Brumas Resort. Tawau, Sabah

Aminuddin and Bryan in Indonesia Surabaya
Mount Bromo 1996

My trip to Java at Mount Bromo Indonesia with the chairman of the Parent Teachers Association of St Patrick Primary School Mr. Aminuddin bin Abdul Karim

Mount Bromo Java Indonesia

Mount Bromo Indonesia with the chairman

KURSUS "PERTUTURAN DIALEK HOKKIEN" BIL. 1/97
14.7.97 HINGGA 2.8.97 DI INTAN K.L.

Duduk Dari Kiri : Rashid B. Bakar, Amy (Malemy), Puan Ong Boeh Hong, En. Tan Kung Chuan, En. Saw Kin Lee, Puan Loh Lee Lee
Cik Wee Sheau Ping, Puan Tan Lay Khoon, Bryaan Paul Lai, Aminah Kassim, Ismail Bin Ahamad.
Baris Tengah Dari Kiri : Norlin Bin Johari, Halim Bin Musa, Wong Ching Sing, Razman Abdullah, Noriah Bt Haji Abd Rahman, Saroji
A/P Kasi, Omar B. Syed Mohamed, Kamaruddin Shukor, Kelingkang Anak Egai, Khalid B Che Rus, Ahmad Sudian Bin Abdullah,
Masor @ Mansor B. Bolkis.
Baris Belakang Dari Kiri : Mohd Fikry B. Haji Abd Samad, Fadzil Muhamad, Che Ab Aziz Bin Daud, Md. Rasid Mustapha, Wong We
Shung, Ahmad Zawawi B Abd Majid, Mohamad Radzi Ishak, Idris B Abdullah.

Hokkien dialect course at Intan KL my final course before my retirement.
The author's third from the right sitting in front..

With all the activities going on at St Patrick, I was not aware that my time was running out and had to ensure the administrative handover was finalized before I left for my compulsory retirement. My final course that the department accorded to me before my final retirement was to learn the Hokian dialect at Intan KL from the 14.7.97 to 2.8.97. Most of those participating were police officers and custom officers from their respective towns in Malaysia

Episode 10

The family bond

*W*ith the blink of an eye, time had just gone by, without us realizing that our nuptials life had finally crossed the silver lining to an unwavering existence. We finally reached a quarter of our marriage life, through trial and tribulation, typical of any couple. A simple gathering to bring families and close friends to commemorate the occasion was held at our house at Kampung Muhiibbahraya, Tawau Sabah.

Portrait from left: Lilian, Paul, Peter my father, Mom Gabriela, Datin Albert Watson and Datuk Albert Watson, Our marriage God Father at our Kampong Muhibbahraya House.

Datuk Albert Watson and his wife from Kunak, and close acquaintances of the family graced the evening. Their presence at the party as well as all my relatives and circle of friends made the party warm, and meaningful

Datuk Hasbullah Taha, the director of education, officers from the Ministry and my former boss Mr. Albert Chia took time away to attend the evening gatherings.

Our special guest the Sabah Director of Education Datuk Sri
Dr Hasbullah bin Taha, the Federal Secretary to the Ministry of
Education, his officers and my former boss Mr. Albert Chia..

Our family friend Mr. Peter Chong and his wife Lucy

My service

$\mathcal{I}$n 1996 I received the education service merit by the Minister of Education. It was handed over by Yang Berhormat Datuk Najib bin Abdul Razak. A gratification by the ministry to provide to long service teachers of the Ministry stationed in Sabah.

The Tawau education officer Encik Mohd Ukong looked on as I received the merit, from the Minister of Education Datuk Najib bin Abdul Razak

Augustine my son and I at the Yang Dipertuan Agong's
Chamber Kuala Lumpur after receiving the long service merit award. PPN

The Sandakan Anzac Memorial Day, Sabah Malaysia

Reminiscence of the past

$\mathcal{T}$he Second World War in 1941 to 1945 had brought some momentous impact to my mother. I was just a baby when my father was taken away by the Japanese and sent to Kuching Prison. He was charged for providing medical aids, to the Allied Prisoner of War interned in Sandakan. He was later released by the Australian Military after the war ended at the end of 1945.

As part of the Remembrance Day, the Sandakan Municipal Council had organized their yearly "lest we forget event". Many of those locals involved in the war were invited to take part in the ceremony. Since my father was no longer available, I was duly invited to speak on his behalf during one of the yearly occasions.

It began in the wee hours of the morning and ended at around nine, followed by the morning high tea.

The Anzac day memorial service at Sandakan Sabah held in the year 2006.

MAJLIS PERBANDARAN SANDA AN

It was a solemn morning, as I addressed the crowd of dignitaries, at the Anzac Memorial Ceremony in Sandakan, Sabah Malaysia.

Those present at the ceremony from left My wife Lilian, Mr. Lagan, Ryan Rowland from Australia, my mother Gabriela Remedia Lobos and Stella Lagan the daughter of Mr. Lagan

The final bugle called to honour those who had given their lives for the sake of peace during the second world war of 1941-1945 in Sandakan Sabah Malaysia

*After the Second World War of 1945 Peter Raymond Lai was awarded
the King's Medal from the Commonwealth of Nation for providing
aid to the Australian and Allied Prisoner of War in Sandakan.*

THE COLONY OF NORTH BORNEO.

Office of the D.M.S. Jesselton.
DMS/47/262/2

21st August, 1947.

Mr. Peter Raymond Lai,
Tongod Dispensary,
S A N D A K A N.

We are advised that you have been
awarded the very high honour of the King's
Medal for Courage in the Cause of Freedom.

Please accept our heartiest personal
congratulations. We thank you also for the
credit you have brought to this department.

COMMONWEALTH OF AUSTRALIA

DEPARTMENT OF THE ARMY
MELBOURNE, AUSTRALIA

No. 75   22nd March 1947.

To Mr. Peter Raymond Lai Kui Fook.
of Civil Hospital.
Sandakan.

The Minister for the Army of the Commonwealth of Australia desires to recognize your
valuable assistance to Australian soldiers during
the War with Japan, 1941-1945, and extends
to you, on behalf of the Commonwealth and
the next-of-kin, most sincere thanks for services
rendered.

Cyril Chambers

MINISTER FOR THE ARMY

Issued at Melbourne.
Countersigned

Past documents of Peter Raymond Lai of North Borneo.

Reminiscence of Tawau first industry

The first ever known local industry that took root in North Borneo was the Silimponpon Coal Mine at Kalabakan village, Tawao North Borneo

The mode of transport for the coal miners at Silimponpon, Kalabakan Tawau (1905-1937)

The Silimponpon coal mine village in Kalabakan hamlet, Tawau, North Borneo. (1905-1937)

The Managerial team of the company and their family at Silimponpon coal mine Kalabakan Tawau North Borneo (1905-1937)

The Silimponpon Coal mine village in the Kalabakan Prefecture, Tawau North Borneo 1905-1937 (now Sabah)

Officials of the Silimponpon coal mine visiting their coal mining enterprise at Kalabakan Prefecture, Tawau North Borneo (1905-1037)

Some of the executives of the coal mine in Silimponpon at Kalabakan Prefecture (1905-1937) Tawau North Borneo (now Sabah).

The Domingo brothers and their family at the
Silimponpon coal mine Kalabakan 1905-1937.

Chinese Marriage ceremony at Silimpoinpon coal mine
in Kalabakan region Tawau North Borneo (1905-1937)
The dress code resembled the Han dynasty era.

Simple marriage amongst the workers also took place at Silimponpon (1905-1937)

The children of the Silimponpon village in 1905-1937

The European miners at work in Silimponpon in Kalabakan area, Tawau North Borneo (1905-1937).

Workers busy at work at the Silimponpon coal mine at Kalabakan Tawau North Borneo

The police contingent at Silimponpon were mostly Sikh from India, under A British officer to ensure law and order and the security of the company.

The final resting place of workers at Silimponpon, Kalabakan Tawau North Borneo (1905-1937)

Closure of Silimponpon mine in 1937

*T*he passage of time had completely wiped out the existence of the mine. For the locals and those not in the picture of the said mine, giving a thought of gratification that such industry could have existed in Tawau would provide some food for thoughts.

By virtue of its right in the history of Tawau, the mine was the catalyst that brought Tawau to the front of rapid development by the influx of thousand of high skill workers throughout the region.

The coal mine had been known to be one of the biggest in the world during that period. It was owned by the London-based Cowie Harbor Coal Company. It started in the year 1905 and provided coal to many steamships that were playing around in this part of the world. In 1937, the company ceased its operation. The company had a workforce of more than 3000 that came from Indonesia, Hong Kong, the Philippines and other regions, that exceed the population of Tawau. With the closure of the coal mine, many of the populace in the mining company settled in Tawau town and took Tawau as their permanent home. The movement of the inhabitants altered the demographic status of Tawau population. The majority of them settled at Jalan Sin On, Jalan Apas and Jalan Kuhara. With this new group of industries, new settlers, Tawau expanded as never seen before, bringing their knowhow and expertise in additional to the British administrative skill from the mining company. Several big plantations such as Borneo Abaca, Mostyn Estate and several other local enterprises sprung up. The mundane life of Tawau had now gradually a thing of the past and the town became a busy barter trade port. Copra, rubber, birds nest, jungle products and others. Most of the products were exported to Hong Kong and other countries whilst China goods began to fill the shelves of the shopkeepers in town. Each Chinese ethnic group that had a strong bond with their country of origin started to open up business according to their forefather's expertise.

*Round timbers ready for export at Wallace Bay. Note the
timbers laid on the sea and the ship ready to load them.*

*F*rom 1963, the timber industry began to spurt upwards as the demand
for the timbers of the world grew tremendously. This economic upturn
brought local enterprise and companies to grow within a short period of
time. The town expanded and previous timber houses manifested into
concrete and permanent structure. However, as a large chunk of the timber
area gradually depleted and unsustainable, the economy of Tawau began
to lose its momentum at a gradual pace. Auspiciously several companies
such as Borneo Alpaca and other Chinese enterprise had embarked on
planting cocoa, rubber on a large scale and were in time to stimulate the
economy. The price of cocoa made an upward trend due to world demand.
Smallholders and some large local companies were saved from insolvency.

The cocoa boom brought great relief to the Tawau region, planting of cocoa
spread like wildfire at every nook and corners of Tawau. The event spurred
the economic boom to the people of Tawau a redeemer to plantations that
had been struggling to put their head up over trouble water. This occurrence
gave them room for some breathing space. That sudden movement in world
commodities gave them a fresh lease of life, and kept many of them from
financial lost. Tawau was once again saved by the turn of events as the

timber industry, the economic lifeline of the populace gradually depleted as the availability of the timber area diminished.

Borneo Abaca and Mostyn Estate, the pioneering plantations formulated by the British government, played an active role in giving jobs to thousands of personals due to the closure of the coal mine. Before the Second World War, several Japanese companies had a foothold in the Tawau region planting jutes and rubber. During the war, the Japanese took control of the whole Borneo region and brought in thousands of Japanese to Tawau to assimilate them with the locals. Most of them were repatriated back to Japan after they lost the war in 1945.

Tawau on the road to recovery.

$\mathcal{T}$he population of Tawau began to grow with migrants coming from Indonesia to take up plantation jobs and investors from West Malaysia buying up lands for plantation, thus began the cocoa boom. Every available land suitable for cocoa planting was snatched up. Rubber trees, coconut trees and other plants were all replaced by cocoa. The whole landscape of Tawau had transformed into a cocoa town.

Typical cocoa plant in Tawau, Sabah

The cocoa research station in Sabah at the Queen Hill Research Station was actively researching on new budded clone, They succeeded and hybrid clone of cocoa seedling were widely provided and sold to farmers and companies at a nominal price. At Borneo Abaca Limited the ever continued research on cocoa had yielded some positive results and high yield cocoa plants were made available to farmers. The golden pods became the highly subject of conversation amongst the plantation owners and local populace of the township.

Every coffee shop during a yam cha time (coffee break) spoke nothing else except the planting of cocoa and its lucrative returns. Those with several hundred acres were called Cocoa King.

Many small holders were fortunate to be part of the craze, although it was only a fractional percentage in the wagon of the cocoa domain. My plot of land which I bought several years ago missed the boat at a high peak. Our main factor that impeded this race was due to financial restrain. With regret I continued to do the best that I had within my government diminutive salary.

It took me several years to generate proper income. Finally, as the whole area was developed, the price of cocoa started to spiral downwards. Farmers could still survive, but on a very thin margin. Saddled by the low price, workers' problem and incomplete infrastructure created an uphill task of maintaining the area. As the months passed by, farmers were counting the days when they could get back their initial outlay and to reimburse the loan which they took from the banks.

While my production increased from month to month, the cocoa price began to slide down progressively, on the verge of touching the red line. We barely survive to stay afloat, as workers problems and shortfall became intolerable. The Malaysian cocoa board set up their office in Tawau and offered assistance and expertise to the local farmers. Seminars were conducted from time to time and small holders were invited to take part and given some assistance in kind such as fertilizers and other relevant materials.

The cocoa pot borers that broke the camel's back

*F*armers were struggling with their farms and barely made ends meet. Cocoa was still the thriving economy, until, an unseen menace that emerged out of the blue.

The farmers were stunned, a threat that came from nowhere. Thousand of acres of cocoa farm were affected and every means at their disposable to contain the new enemy. The agriculture department and the cocoa research station drastically tried to curb the problem but in vain. Every method was employed in the field. Young thumb size fruits were stripped off from every tree, carpet spraying and bagging was initiated promptly. The all out war had begun, but the extreme action by the agriculture department failed to curb the menace.

The farmers had to lick their wounds and tried to survive at every means. The menace that came out of the blue created the cocoa industry in Tawau to a breaking point of no return.

The menace was caused by the cocoa pod borer, a mosquito like insect that bored into the young thumb size pods. Prior to this unexpected threat, the disease that affected the present cocoa plant such as black pots and other root disease was minimal and of no great alarmed. The agriculture department and the cocoa research station at Quoin Hill were kept on their toes monitoring the disease occurrence. The small holders took great care to upkeep the cocoa farm, and provide good husbandry maintenance, but had lost the war against this outbreak. As the epidemic continued unabated, the workers had a hard time to dislodge the hard clustered beans.

With the price sliding down to its lowest point, and the plague of the cocoa pod borer intensified, the industry lost its lustre and farmers began to look for some other alternative to control their losses. Most of the areas at Sin On Tiku finally had a different scenic view. The cocoa plants that were once monopolized the whole scenario as far as the eye could see had been turned into the oil palm landscape. Those with bank loan had to trade away their farm to minimize their losses. Lastly, many of the small holders at Sin On Tiku began to change their farm and the land area of cocoa farms reduced dramatically to just ten percent of what it was once had. Some areas that remained standing were those that belonged to Teck Guan Company that needed the area to supply the raw materials to their chocolate factory at Tanjung Batu. They too experienced the pinch and had to import cocoa from neighbouring countries.

The unexpected redeemer

Gradually, as the years passed by, a silver lining emerged. The oil palm industry getting its momentum and the past issue that farmers faced had finally been solved.

A decade ago, oil palm had been planted in large scale in Sandakan and Tawau by large corporations. It was undertaken by big companies with strong financial backing to feed their oil mill factory. Small farmers were not apt to venture due to its intensive nature of the operation. There were many factors, one had to consider before one could undertake such a project unless supported by big financial outlay.

The oil palm farm in Tawau

In the past, pollination of the flowers had to be done manually by hand that required a great work force. The transport problem that needed to be delivered to the factory at a long distance and waiting in the queue would be another factor that discouraged many small farmers to shy away from planting oil palm in their plot of land.

However, in the year 2000, the end game in the oil palm plantation began to shift. There was no more manual pollination required. That little insect called weevil could do the task which had been applied in Johor successfully. Finally the agriculture department took it to Sabah and applied it in the plantation with great success.

The price of the commodities began to spiral upwards to a heartening price never seen before, encouraging farmers to replace their cocoa plants with oil palm without any compulsion. The introduction of the weevil insect, culminating with the high price boosted the oil palm industry, that farmers in Tawau once again scrambled into the oil palm wagon as they did in the period of the cocoa boom. Acreage after acreage of cocoa farms were converted into oil palm trees. The excavator operator was kept busy as they began terracing the hilly areas of Sin On. In 2006, I finally succumb to the trend and abandoned my cocoa farm and instead try my luck into the oil palm adventure. Two visionary companies built their collection centre, just a few kilometres away from the Sin On area that made it convenient for farmers around the Sin On prefecture to sell their products. Tawau was once again relieved by this unexpected event. Shop houses and housing estate sprouted like no body's business. Land and residential lot began to be expensive, beyond the reach of many wage earners.

In conclusion

*W*ith the additional influx of the Silimponpon workforce to Tawau town, many skilled workers of different nationalities were added to the populace of Tawau.

My footprint was felt in Tawau in the fifties when I was just seven years old and studied in Holy Trinity School. It was just a small hamlet with an inhabitant that mostly came from neighbouring countries. What attracted them to this town? The Japanese were heavily involved in the jute plantation and other enterprise before the war, attracted by the suitable soil composition. The Japanese present before the war, culminating long lasting names such as Kuhara, Kabota, Dr Yamamoto etc. We're still part of the landmark in the district of Tawau.. After the Second World War, most of the Japanese populace was repatriated back to Japan and the North Borneo became a colony of the British Empire.

The first Japanese hospital was situated just before the Government Secondary School at Kampong Jawa crossed the Tawau river and a bridge built by the military in 1964 called Tungku Osman Bridge

The custom department by the shore

*The shop houses constructed of palm leaves constructed just after
the Second World War, but was burnt down in 1953.*

*The first Tawau Airport at Jalan Utara. The boy standing is
the author, Bryan Paul Lai taken with a Kodak camera*

The Tawau new modern airport built fifty years later, taken with a canon digital camera.

Tawau in the 21ˢᵗ century view from Lay Hotel Tawau

Tawau is growing rapidly in the 21st century. View from LAY Hotel

For the people of Tawau, luck had been on their side throughout the years of its emergence.. When the economy was down, some events just came out of the blue and brought them back to life. After the silimponpon coal mine, timber had been the main revenue of growth for many years and as timber began unsustainable with its vast forest disappeared, other commodities took its place like the Cocoa Boom and when the commodities reversed its market price which put so many companies and farmers in jeopardy, the oil palm industries suddenly took an upward trend and provide the necessary impetus for the financial circulation of cool hard currency, just in the nick of time for another redeemer giving a helping hand to the populace. Will this luck continue to bring Tawau to a greater height and turn Tawau

Town into a metropolitan city that we could be proud of! When the British governed our county, they left a legacy of good government which Sabahan is now emulating its heritage.

Beside the easy going populace, Tawau had been marred by a fire mishap that destroyed the whole town in 1953. It was then rebuilt and concrete shop houses began to rise. Throughout the years, many wooden shops took its toil from the scourge of fires, but transform into a more permanent building being as it stood today. Travelling had to be done either by air or ship. There were no roads connecting to the various towns in Sabah. This infrastructure only began in earnest in the seventies.

The first parish Priest and his early flock.Rev Fr Stooter. Photo taken in 1922 at the Parish Building of Holy Trinity Church Tawao North Borneo

Several of the pictures whose family are now staying in Tawau such as Voo Kon Hoi, The Domingoes, The Tan family. (Previously working at the Silimponpon coal mine.)

Schools had played a very important role in the development of Tawau. Top on the list in the fifties were the Holy Trinity Catholic Mission (1922) and St Patrick Anglican school, several Chinese schools such as Sin Hua and Yuk Chin and the Malay vernacular school previously located on the sea front that provided the town with its educated workforce. In 1963, when Sabah became independent, and joined Malaysia, the locals then recognized the Hugh potential of its natural resources

The Mamut Copper mine in Ranau and the timber industry under Yayasan Sabah had generated the economy of the State of Sabah. Tawau became the epic centre in the commodity market. In correlation to this development, more shop houses started to sprout and the housing industry developed unhindered

I strongly believe that Tawau still has its huge potential from its untapped resources that need to be exploited. If the Tarakan town close to Tawau has an oil field, its not far fetch to presume that beneath the soil of Kalabakan, Tawau also has a vast amount of gas or the hidden gold treasure beneath the soil at Mount Wulldersdorf Balung. Optimistically, that would be the next economic growth that would bring Tawau forward in the coming years to come. We beg and hope that personal extremist that had been looming in our nation was only a diminishing cloud. We require to nurture and defend the bastion of the principle of law and parliamentary procedure so that no bigotry elements could create anarchy and destroy the country which we totally enjoy.

The second of a new time frame had finally got up with me and my retirement at age fifty five was just round the nook. After more than 29 years working as a teacher and administrator, I had to go along to keep myself realistically and retire gracefully for the coming years to pass.

On my retirement on 29 June 1998, I was very surprised to get several letters from my own pupils depicting their feelings and compassionate. To my students, who spent some effort to compose a few lines of admiration from their little loving kindness, my grateful thanks. To all the staff of my school my apology in case of negative unintended words that came out during the tenure of my responsibilities in the school. Just to make a note that these students who wrote the simple notes came from these benevolent children, which are getting rare in our society of today. Will our leaders of tomorrow ever realized that the future of our nation will entirely depend on the populace with holistic kindness in the heart with their fellow being.

My purpose of putting it here was to thank these students of mine and to make their names known for our younger generation to emulate and to be known that caring feeling is not dead yet. Your discretion is needed to draw any conclusion.

Finally, I would like to thank all those who had given me the encouragement to finish this historical diary of what life was all about in Tawau and to all those that had contributed pictures and words of encouragement, especially to Mary Domingo, pictures of Silimponpon, Mr Colin Rose of Tasmania pictures of the British involvement during the Confrontation of 1963 to 1966 between Malaysia and Indonesia, Mr Francis Anthony, pictures of Wallace Bay during the timber era Mary Lu for the youth seminars in Sandakan, Labuan and Papar, and Annie Hee photos of yesteryear, to George Chang of Tawau who provided several pictures had been my sincere friend since those school days and finally to Marguerite my daughter of Kota Kinabalu who gave some positive comments...

Family gathering at Suria Shopping Mall Sabah 2012

P 49: Picture of my family taken in the year 2012 at
Suria Mall Kota Kinabalu Sabah Malaysia.
1) Marguerite Lai spouse Mr Nicholas Kau Children:
Ryan, Brandon Jordan and Chloe
2) Augustine Lai spouse Josephine Lee.
3) Sharonita Lai spouse Liew Chi Chau Children: Michelle and Derek
4) Abigail Lai Spouse Kevyn Chan Child: Tristan Chan

Bryan Paul Lai.SP,PPN,ADK
Email:sinontiku@gmail.com
Author

Printed in the United States
By Bookmasters